LEUKEMIA CHICK

MY JOURNEY WITH THE BIG C - A STORY OF HOPE

SARAH MURRAY

Leukemia Chick
Copyright © 2024 by Sarah Murray

All rights reserved. No part of this publication may be reproduced, distributed, or transmitted in any form or by any means, including photocopying, recording, or other electronic or mechanical methods, without the prior written permission of the author, except in the case of brief quotations embodied in critical reviews and certain other non-commercial uses permitted by copyright law.

tellwell

Tellwell Talent
www.tellwell.ca

ISBN
978-1-77941-618-6 (Paperback)
978-1-77941-619-3 (eBook)

DISCLAIMER

One thing to know about my aunt is that she was an amazing gift-giver, so it's no surprise that the last gift she gave was the best of all—her book. She led her life with courage and generosity despite her encounters with cancer—or The Big C. She took life's setbacks with more resilience than the average person and was an amazing example to us all.

But she was not a medical practitioner.

Anyone with health concerns should not look to this book for medical advice. Since the time of my aunt's many treatment protocols, medicine has undergone significant advancements. While many procedures described in this book were practised in a major children's hospital in the 1980s, they are not meant in any way to describe today's treatments.

Health care has changed, but the adversity my aunt faced has not.

The book is not a medical guide, but it is a memoir that describes her personal reflections and interpretations at key points in her life. These experiences are shared from her perspective based on her personal memories—the highs and lows of living with cancer. I hope you find meaning and enjoyment in her stories as she paints the tapestry that is her memoir.

- Breanne Murray
2024-02-14

TABLE OF CONTENTS

FOREWORD 1
PROLOGUE 3
Chapter 1 THE 2ND AVENUE GANG 4
Chapter 2 THE FIRST TIME AROUND 14
Chapter 3 A PRECIPICE LOOMS 24
Chapter 4 GOD CHOOSES THE ZONK 39
Chapter 5 BABUDEEP: BLEMISHED,
                UNIBROWED & DISTENDED 50
Chapter 6 BABUDEEP: BLEMISHED PHANTOM 56
Chapter 7 BABUDEEP: BARBIE-ARMED &
                ENFLAMED-EYED 63
Chapter 8 KUDOS TO CAREGIVERS 74
Chapter 9 IT WAS THE BEST OF TIMES 95
Chapter 10 IT WAS THE WORST OF TIMES 108
Chapter 11 EUROPEAN VACATIONS 119
Chapter 12 SCHOOL DAZE 141
Chapter 13 ANIMANIAC 147
Chapter 14 SHE WORKS HARD FOR THE MONEY 157
Chapter 15 TAPESTRY 162

Chapter 16 THE TONIC OF SPECIAL FRIENDSHIPS..... 173
Chapter 17 FAITH, FRIENDSHIP AND GOD...................... 178
EPILOGUE 187
AFTERWORD... 188
ACKNOWLEDGEMENTS 189
ABOUT THE AUTHOR 191

FOREWORD

"I think she's stopped breathing," I said to my son Ted.

I rang for the nurse, who confirmed it. Thus the end came—peacefully and without pain—to a life filled with struggles and tests, blessings and rich victories.

Sarah was my hero, and I'd had the privilege of being her father for over fifty-one years. Diagnosed with leukemia when she was only fourteen, then losing the battle against cancer—The Big C, as she called it—at age fifty-one, her time on earth was a testimony to how one can grab hold of life, despite much opposition, and wring out every bit of living possible. She fought hard to live a "normal" life, and she used every resource available to her to do so.

But now the struggle was over.

I miss her deeply and will continue to for the remainder of my life. This is her story, offered that you may be challenged to confront the many perils life may throw at you and encouraged to know that you can live a life of blessing—sometimes because of, and sometimes in spite of—those perils.

Gary Murray
2023-09-24

PROLOGUE

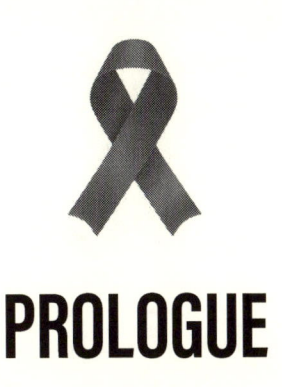

SPRING 1986. I WAS OUT OF the hospital after completing my initial chemo and radiation treatments to get my leukemia diagnosis into remission. I was feeling particularly freakish that day as I rode my bike up and down the dead-end street in front of my house. There were some younger kids around who were whispering and acting astonished that the "sick girl" was able to ride a bike so soon after being in the hospital. At some point, my oldest brother, who I'll call Ted, came outside and said something like, "Hey, Leukemia Chick."

Now you may wonder why he used those words. Was it because he wanted to insult me? Did he want to put me down in front of others? Or was it for some other reason? Well, let me tell you my story. It's about the highs and lows, the successes and failures, the blessings and blows of me, the Leukemia Chick.

CHAPTER ONE:
THE 2ND AVENUE GANG

Location, Location, Location

My family moved to Shelburne, Ontario, population 2,500, in 1972 when my dad secured a job as head of English at the local high school. I was six months old, and I had two older brothers: one (whom I'll call Mike) aged two, and the other (whom I'll call Ted) aged five. We also had a family dog named Taffy. My mom stayed home full-time with the rug rats until a few years later when she started working part-time as a registered nurse (RN) at the local hospital.

Looking back on my childhood, the word "idyllic" comes to mind. Our big old Victorian house was ideally situated on a dead-end street within easy walking distance to the high school. There were eight houses on our side of the street and seven on the other. Five of the houses were occupied by elderly widows, and retired couples lived across the street and on the right side of our house. Middle-aged couples with teenagers, and young couples with kids near my and my brothers' ages rounded off the 2nd Avenue West occupants. I became best friends with a boy (whom I'll call Shawn) who was one year ahead of me in school and lived across the street. We were among the younger kids, and when the older kids weren't telling us to get lost, we loved to hang around with them, like a gang — the 2nd Avenue Gang.

Living on a dead-end street allows you to use the actual street as part of your playground. Ted loved to play street hockey with his friends and with Taffy the Wonder Dog. He even let his little sister join in at times. The street was also ideal for a game where the appointed leader stands about twenty feet away from the others and calls out the initials of a TV show. Both the person who correctly guesses the name of the show and the leader start running to the opposite side and back again. The fastest person either remains the leader or takes over as the leader. While it was a fun game, determining a winner could turn into a huge argument. Someone always walked away in a huff when accused of starting to run while giving the answer as opposed to waiting to hear if the answer was correct.

Street games were interrupted only occasionally when someone shouted, "Car!"; however, for a short time each weekday, the street turned into a busy raceway. Train tracks for the Toronto, Grey and Bruce railway ran about a hundred feet away from the end of the street. At the first sound of the whistle, people emerged from their houses, some running at full pace towards the sound, hoping to arrive in time for the conductor to return their enthusiastic waves and pull a special *toot! toot!* just for them. Remember the show *Fantasy Island* where Tattoo would shout, "The plane! The plane!" as visitors were about to arrive? Imagine mothers and children running down the street shouting, "The train! The train!" Now that's small-town living!

Criminal Activity

We in the 2nd Avenue Gang were big fans of the game hide-and-seek, especially at night. When my parents settled in to watch the news after dinner, my brothers and I were off to find adventure outside. These were the days when you'd just say, "I'm going out!" with no details required. I had the earliest curfew by far—like an hour earlier than my best friend Shawn who was only six months older than me. I knew what time I needed to be home, but I always waited until my dad would open the side door and yell my name. Once I heard it, the race was on to get home before I heard him call a second time, for I had experienced the consequences of dawdling.

These were also the days when many people didn't feel the need to lock their doors before going to bed (let alone during the day). I don't think it crossed anyone's mind that their kids might be in danger from strangers lurking around in the dark. Their concern was mainly their kids coming home in time so they didn't have to go outside to look for them. Our main concern was getting back to "home" (the streetlight pole at the end of our driveway) before the person who was "it." Others had concerns as well. Namely those who happened upon dark figures hiding in their window wells, sheds and porches. These were mainly elderly neighbours who weren't happy that we were allowed to rove around the hood so "late" at night.

There was another night-time activity we engaged in that was a lot more gang-like than trespassing on the elderly neighbours' properties. In case you're not familiar, nicky nicky nine doors involves kids knocking on doors or ringing doorbells and running away before someone answers. We'd "put up our dukes" for a round of eeny, meeny, miny, moe to see who had to run to the door. One time when Mike lost, he didn't make it off the property before someone answered. Knowing he was about to get caught, my clever brother laid down on his back and said he was "star gazing." Who would believe that a sweet young kid like him would be the perpetrator of such a cruel trick?

In the winter, the gang took advantage of early darkness with an equally stupid (perhaps stupider) activity. Night gave us the cover we needed from unsuspecting drivers after we made piles of rock-hard snowballs to throw at cars. The younger kids, like myself, were more of an accessory to this crime as our snowball-throwing arms weren't up to snuff. There was a stop sign at the junction of 2nd Avenue West and Gordon Street. As cars approached, the big kids would pelt them with snowballs. Some kids would climb on the roof of the house closest to the stop sign and throw snowballs from there just in case someone got out of their car to catch the culprits.

Gordon Street didn't have much night-time traffic, so one night the older kids got bored and decided to find a street with more cars. Of course, they chose the busiest street in Shelburne. All was well until a car that had a police car behind it was hit. Everyone scrambled to avoid getting caught, but this time I was the one who didn't get away. I don't recall what I said when the policeman pulled up beside me and rolled down the window. I couldn't have been any older than nine, so I probably started to cry and proclaim my innocence so I wouldn't get tossed in the clink. It's better that I was caught instead of one of the older kids as I have a feeling that the cop would have driven them home to have a talk with their parents. The rest of the gang members would have been ratted out and punished, so I'd say my brothers and I avoided a long grounding.

Off-Street Hijinks

Another amazing aspect of our neighbourhood was Hyland Park. It was like a large extension of my backyard, and I spent hours hanging out there with the gang. The town's public pool was located in the park about twenty feet away from the gravel road outside our back gate. There was also a large cement wading pool with a fountain in the middle where we splashed around on hot summer days.

The high school football field was the divider between two playgrounds. The playground closest to my back gate had a metal contraption we called the "octopus" (although it had only six "legs"). We could climb up any of the arched ladders that merged at the top and sit as kings and queens, surveying our surrounding kingdom. The octopus was also great for hanging upside down, but not so great if you stuck your tongue on it in the winter.

My favourite was the large swing set with four baby swings and four big-kid swings. The big-kid swing seats were long, flat and made of rubber. The chains were sturdy and hung the perfect height from the ground. We didn't give a hoot about safety, but the swings were safe to sit or stand on. I saw a recent picture of the current swings, and while they're still long and made of rubber, they're saggy—no more standing.

While this playground had a much better swing set, the playground on the other side of the football field had an awesome slide. We often ran up the slide, then slid down it, skipping the ladder (much to the dismay of other kids waiting for their turn). If we were wearing shorts, we had to slide down legs up on our bums, as bare skin doesn't slide well and metal slides can get very hot in the summer sun. The playground also included a public pavilion filled with picnic tables where people often gathered on Sundays after church to enjoy food and fellowship. Beyond the pavilion was the community baseball diamond which was the "official" diamond where teams who wore uniforms played—the small-town big leagues.

The 2nd Avenue Gang was a competitive bunch, and our preferred swing set was the location for shoe-kicking competitions. We'd jump on the swings, four at a time, and start pumping madly. When we were ready, we'd slide our heels out of one shoe, then shoot one leg forward, releasing our shoes like we were firing off a cannonball. Then we'd start again, often placing the other shoe on the same foot if we thought we'd get a better result. After everyone finished kicking off both shoes, we'd jump off the swings and run to see whose shoes landed the farthest away. However, some of us didn't have far to run as our shoes either fell off before launching or we'd swung our legs so high that they landed behind us. Eventually, I got the knack and became a pretty decent shoe-kicker.

Now even though I was one of the younger kids, there was one swing-set competition, actually more of a dare, where I thought I could strut my stuff. I was pretty much a fearless child—maybe more stupid than fearless—but I wanted to prove myself to the older kids. The basic challenge was to prove who had the guts to swing as high as they could and then jump off. While many of us younger kids had done it before, we weren't swinging nearly as high as the big kids. When it was my turn, I pumped and pumped until the chains on the swing began to bend (which I soon learned means that you're swinging too high), then launched myself off the swing. When I landed, I thought I had broken my feet—the pain level was 100 on a scale of 1-10. I didn't break anything, but lesson learned.

Being Schooled: Past and Present

The Shelburne Pioneer Museum, an open-air museum established in 1963, was located just outside Hyland Park's grounds. Several buildings, including a home, a barn and an Orange Lodge, were filled with artifacts skillfully displayed to reflect the rural and agricultural heritage of the region. There was also a caboose to climb on and let our imaginations run wild. Visitors had to pay to get in, but Shawn and I could visit pretty much whenever we wanted for free. We became so familiar with the artifacts and the history behind them that we would act as tour guides for visitors. The Pioneer Museum has long since closed, but the artifact collection was officially donated to the county in 1988. This collection, along with parts of some of the buildings, now reside inside and on the grounds of the Dufferin Museum, located on Airport Road in Mulmur. What a blessing to be able to revisit wonderful childhood memories.

Across the street from Hyland Park, a gravel road led into one side of Shelburne Junior Public School (SJPS). This school was old—and I mean old—like the large brick schools you see in history books or horror movies. It was established in 1898, complete with a belfry above the main entrance, cloakrooms and metal chute fire escapes (more fun than any of the playground equipment). The basement area was all stone and it had a freaky storeroom where a classmate and I were sometimes sent to retrieve supplies for the teacher. Too short to reach the light switch, we were convinced that a deranged lunatic was waiting to jump out and kill us. The school janitor lived a few doors down from Shawn's house and the 2nd Avenue kids were his favourites. He even allowed us to accompany him to the belfry and ring the ancient bell. I attended the school from kindergarten to Grade 3, but it was no longer a school to me when classes ended, it was 2nd Avenue Gang turf.

In the summer we played baseball in the small, beat-up diamond located in one corner of the schoolyard. Even with the whole gang present, there were only eight of us, but we still made it work—four kids per team, the pitcher and hitter doubling as the back catcher, and the three kids on base doubling as outfielders. We started with a "schoolyard pick," youngest kids picked last, of course. I didn't care, I was just happy to play with the big kids. Some of the other younger kids weren't as keen as I was on the game, and when they weren't hitting, they'd often sit down in the field and pick dandelions. The older kids were into the game, and the boys were pretty heavy hitters. One day when she was positioned to catch the ball, an older girl got hit straight in the mouth. She must have had strong teeth because when we ran to see if she was OK, nothing was missing, there was just a lot of blood.

Fiddle Dee Dee

Shelburne was also known as Fiddleville. Every August, scads of people throughout North America arrived in our sleepy town for the Canadian Open Old Time Fiddler's Contest and several days of rootin'-tootin' events. Hyland Park housed the trailers that crammed into every nook and cranny. My parents (and many of our neighbours) were not fans of fiddle week, especially the sounds of fiddle music and drunken parties at all hours of the day and night. Then there were the drunk partiers who would stagger into our backyards or just assume they could cut through them. We, however, thought it was cool, and when my parents didn't schedule a family vacation to escape it, the 2nd Avenue Gang had a lot of fun during fiddle week.

I was never a fan of fiddle music either, but we loved to watch the parade, and Shawn's house was ideally situated on the parade's path. We loved the parade cause, well—it's a parade, and doesn't everyone love a parade (especially when you have a front row seat)? But the parade was also a moneymaker. Shawn and I knew that people would be walking by his house in droves, so if ever there was a time to set up a lemonade stand, this was it. We actually sold freshie (water added to a drink mix that was mainly sugar) instead of lemonade, and sometimes extended the menu to include freezies—long tubes of sugary, fruit-flavoured ice.

Shawn and I made a decent buck and we spent it all at the O & J, a convenience store that sold every cavity-causing candy known. Remember Fun Dip? Pure sugar bliss!

There was also a fortune to be made when fiddle week was over. When the trailers rolled out, a bevy of beer bottles were left behind. With dollar signs in our eyes, the 2nd Avenue Gang scrambled to collect every last bottle we could find. I don't recall how much money we made, but it seemed like less of a fortune when we had to divide it up among each gang member. Still, we were as happy as the drunken campers.

Cheers

The 2nd Avenue Gang's turf was expansive: A dead-end street, two park playgrounds, a museum and the entire school grounds were at our disposal. There was always something to do and someone around to do it with. We were extremely blessed kids. The school holds especially precious memories for me. After it burned down in the mid-nineties, I was never able to bring myself to drive by its former location. It's been replaced with numerous houses to accommodate the rapidly growing population. In fact, Shelburne is now the second fastest growing town in Canada, with a current population of 10,249.

When I think about small-town living, the phrase "everybody knows your name" is the one that sticks in my mind. This isn't a bad thing; actually, for the most part, it's kinda nice and creates a friendly, homey atmosphere. However, a lot of people also like to know everybody's business, and as word spreads, truth can get distorted. When everybody knows your name, anything out of the norm (punny?) that happens to someone, especially a kid, singles them out as "that boy" or "that girl" (usually by well-meaning people). When I was fourteen, something out of the norm happened to me and I soon became "that girl" (someone once called me "the girl with the problem"). My idyllic world came crashing down.

Yes, the lows are looming.

CHAPTER TWO:
THE FIRST TIME AROUND

Something's Rotten in the State of Denmark

March Break, 1986. I was fourteen years old and in Grade 8. Midway through the break I was at the high school tennis courts with Shawn hitting balls against the wall. Before long I became unusually tired and sat down on the grass to wait for my energy to return. But it never did. In fact, I was completely spent after less than half an hour of moderate exertion. While I rested, I thought about how I hadn't had much energy for the last few days, but this day was so much worse.

I made up an excuse to leave and collapsed on the family room couch when I got home. For some reason I started to feel my neck around the jawline, and I thought I felt something that wasn't normally there. This scared me and I called for my mom to come and check it out. She also became concerned and knew I needed to see a doctor ASAP.

I figured I had mono, as I knew it was connected with extreme fatigue. My mom also mentioned mono, but what she didn't verbalize was that her RN mind told her a lump in the lymph nodes could be a sign of The Big C. A doctor examined me and ordered some blood tests, and my Spidey senses told me this was much more serious than mono.

Suddenly, mono became something I wished for instead of dreaded.

An eternity later, I was sitting in our family doctor's office with my parents waiting for the test results. When the doctor appeared, he didn't come right out and say the word "cancer," but he did make it clear that my condition was serious.

I don't recall whether it was the same or next day when my parents and I travelled to Sick Kids Hospital in Toronto. I felt so fatigued that going through hours of registration, more blood tests and waiting to see an oncologist was just a blur. However, I soon perked up when I met my new oncologist (I'll call him Dr. S). This must have been what it was like for new army recruits when they first met their sergeant. Dr. S was stern, serious and somewhat scary, so what was he doing working in a children's hospital? Little did I know that this brilliant man, in whose capable hands I'd be placing my teenage life, had a teddy bear heart inside his army sergeant exterior.

Following a quick introduction, he told us that my most recent test results confirmed I had The Big C: acute lymphocytic leukemia (ALL). His demeanour lightened somewhat when he said that ALL was the most common and most treatable form of leukemia, but my mind shut down at "leukemia." He could have started singing the national anthem in pig Latin while standing on his head and I wouldn't have noticed.

I'd heard of leukemia and I was pretty sure that it related to the blood. I recalled seeing a TV movie where the main character had leukemia, but his initial symptoms were severe nosebleeds. In my sheltered small-town life, I'd only known of one person near my age who had The Big C. He was the younger brother of a classmate, and the Shelburne grapevine switched into overdrive when it became known that a young local boy was diagnosed with bone cancer. My diagnosis was gonna be even bigger news; not one, but two local kids diagnosed with The Big C and in the same year, to boot!

I was whisked to a room on the ninth floor cancer ward. My dad drove back to Shelburne to pack a suitcase for me and my mom and let my brothers know what was going on. My mom stayed with me and tried to relieve my scared and confused young mind. Once I calmed down and my mind could handle it, I learned more about ALL. I found out it occurs when the bone marrow produces an abnormal amount of immature white blood cells, called lymphocytes, that prevent healthy white blood cells from being made. As normal blood counts drop, life-threatening symptoms can occur, including infections that don't go away or keep coming back, and frequent or severe bleeding. I also found out that ALL is one of the four most common types of childhood cancer and the survival rate is much higher for children than adults.

In 1986, ALL was treated aggressively with chemotherapy and radiation. If treatment was effective, it would kill the lymphocytes; however, some existing healthy white blood cells would also be killed. Lowered white blood cell counts meant lowered immunity, so I needed to stay away from sick people and large crowds whenever possible. How does one avoid sick people while staying at Sick Kids? Once treatment started, the toxic invasion would hit my body hard, so I'd be in bed a lot anyway. I was told that some days would be better than others and I'd be OK to get up and walk around the ward. If my blood counts stabilized, I could venture out to the cafeteria, and later outside.

La-La Land

These potent treatments caused a lot of nausea and lowered my immunity, which made way for painful infections. There were, however, ways to combat nausea and pain, and I was introduced to the wonderful world of opioids. I'd taken regular and extra strength Gravol and Tylenol, but these drugs were, like, heavy-duty, man. I'm talking intense side effects.

My least favourite drug was meperidine, an opioid analgesic used to help relieve moderate to severe pain. I was often given it when my chemotherapy treatment was going to be particularly heavy. I suppose it relieved any pain, but I didn't notice because I was transported into la-la land once it entered my bloodstream. This wasn't the pleasant zone with tangerine trees and marmalade skies; rather, menacing figures and men glowing green tried to convince me they weren't in my head. Instead of getting drowsy and falling into a peaceful slumber, I would sit in bed, tense and anxious, my eyes darting around the room trying to identify the intruders. I was in a constant state of unease, feeling out of control and unable to rest.

One night after a heavy dose of meperidine, I was visited by another resident from the unpleasant side of la-la land. My mom was staying with me that night, and while she slept, I discovered a tiny fluorescent green man moving around on the far side of my room. I was convinced the figure was not only real but up to no good, so I awoke my poor mom and pleaded for her to confront the intruder. She was skilled at calming me down, and Mr. Green split, but not before leaving me with a gift to unwrap a few hours later. As the drug started to wear off, I started to puke—a predictable and terrifying pattern.

All of these shenanigans left me wondering which was the lesser of the two evils, pain or meperidine?

My opioid of choice became morphine. In the previous chapter, I talked about the off-the-charts pain I experienced after foolishly jumping off a swing at an extreme altitude. This pain, however, was fleeting and I was soon back on my feet, raring to go. When I developed an infection called pleurisy during my treatments, my pain level broke the scale. Pleurisy causes inflammation of layers of tissue that line the inner side of the chest cavity and surround the lungs, leading to sharp chest pain that makes breathing difficult. This pain only subsided when Mr. Morphine came to the rescue and took me to the pleasant side of la-la land. I was one happy camper. Anyone who entered my room was beautiful. Everyone on TV was beautiful. The TV was beautiful, my bed was beautiful, my fingers were beautiful. Best of all, I felt completely in control and at ease. Furthermore, I didn't puke after the drug started to wear off. However, unlike meperidine, morphine left me wanting more, and this feeling helped me gain some understanding of how people become addicted to drugs.

Infections weren't the only thing that caused pain. There was also the dreaded lumbar puncture (Lp), a.k.a. a spinal tap. This is where they insert a long needle between two vertebrae of the lower back and into the spinal cord to remove a sample of cerebrospinal fluid. In the case of ALL patients, the fluid is tested to see if any blood cancer cells are present. Before the procedure begins, patients must be lying on their side in a tight fetal position to open up the space between the vertebrae, making it easier to extract the fluid.

Sound painful? You don't know the half of it.

Dr. S. liked to get procedures done as quickly and efficiently as possible, so there was no waiting for an anesthetic to do its job. As soon as I was in position, and with little warning, he would plunge that horse needle into my back. My mom held my hand and kept my body in place as I winced in pain, wondering what this lunatic had against pain relief. However, after a couple of future pokes, it became clear that Dr. S was neither a lunatic nor someone who took pleasure in others' pain. He was actually an Lp master, and I was soon convinced that bypassing the anesthetic was the better practice.

I'd Rather Be a Wallflower

By June I was in remission, free from The Big C, with safe blood counts. However, while I was about to be sprung from the joint, my treatments were far from over. I would be starting a three-year maintenance protocol as an outpatient. Visits to Sick Kids for treatments would be frequent at first and then taper off as the years progressed.

School was almost out, and there was no point in my returning for the remaining couple of weeks before summer break. I figured that this protocol would work out fine for me, but only for a few short months until I started high school in September. I was already grossly insecure due to my "that girl" status in the community, and my insecurity was coupled with anxiety each time I thought about how I'd be noticeably absent from my afternoon classes each time my mom plucked me from school to drive me to Sick Kids for treatment. My blood would also be tested regularly at a lab in Shelburne Hospital, and if the counts were too low, I couldn't go to school at all. I cringed at the thought of standing out even more when I'd be noticeably absent from school for days, maybe even weeks.

While I couldn't do anything about this treatment protocol further damaging my fragile ego, I could do something about my appearance. Chemotherapy and radiation had taken their toll on my once long, thick hair, and although I didn't lose it all, it wasn't fit to be seen by anyone but my doctors, nurses and parents. My hair was even off limits to very close friends. I was among those teenage girls who was uber-focused on my looks, and my gigantic ego held strong against darkening the high school doors with my hair in its current state. Hats and scarves were out, but bucket hats and bandanas were OK for the time being—anything to help me feel as normal as possible among my peers.

My first day of high school was quickly approaching, so it was the time to get wiggie w'it.

Although I wanted a wig, I was not the least bit keen on shopping for one. I didn't want to show my sparse locks to strangers, and I was sure that the store would be filled with people who would stare at me and give me piteous looks that said, "Poor thing, she's so young." I hoped—but wasn't convinced—that I'd find something close to my natural hair colour. I didn't want one that looked like the cheap wigs you buy for costumes or the wigs and toups I'd seen nursing home residents wearing.

I couldn't have been more wrong.

The process was discreet, and neither the customers nor the salespeople made me feel like a freak. I didn't know you could get wigs made out of human hair or that the vast range of colours allows for an almost perfect match. I left the store with a human hair wig in a colour I was pleased with. The wig wasn't pre-styled, rather it was long and straight so my hairdresser could style it pretty much any way I wanted.

Evil Monarchs

On my first day of high school, I was happy with how my hairdresser had styled my wig and I'd even bought some barrettes to hold the sides back when I wanted to change things up a little. I believed family and friends who told me how real it looked and that anyone who didn't know me would never guess my hair wasn't real.

However, neither my sweet wig nor my flattering first-day-of-school outfit were enough to shoo away the butterflies in my stomach. These weren't the sweet little creatures that followed Snow White around. They were mean, demonic butterflies who sought my demise. Let's face it, I was convinced people would figure out that I had to be wearing a wig—duh! I think it's true, especially when you're young and naïve, that the less you know about something, the more distorted your perception of it can become. Some of my friends had told me that although they were doing their best to dispel them, there were several rumours running around about me.

I knew there would be awkwardness and I'd get a lot of stares, mainly because that's how I'd likely react if the shoe was on the other foot. I started to hope that something would happen to someone else—not something bad, just small-town newsworthy enough to take the spotlight off of me.

I had been filling my head with negative scenarios, each one worse than the other, since I opened my eyes in the morning. By the end of my first class, these thoughts had travelled to my stomach and I was forced to rush to the bathroom and barf. I barely made it to the bathroom after my second class. I went home for lunch to freshen up, and I barfed again. I had to excuse myself part way through third class, but I made it to the end of fourth class. On

Wednesday, the evil butterflies were starting to fly away, as I only barfed twice. On Thursday, I was down to once, and by Friday, the butterflies from hell were gone.

Thankfully, this was an isolated week of barfing. I still had some anxiety, but my stomach became a haven for much nicer butterflies. The main culprit of my extreme anxiety turned out to be my wig. Yes, I was happy with it and I was slowly becoming convinced that it looked real. In fact, a few weeks into school, Mike, now in Grade 11, told me how a classmate commented to him on how fast my hair had grown back. Nevertheless, I still kept getting this nagging feeling that somehow it was going to fall off and reveal the horror underneath. Perhaps someone would pull it, run into it or it would get caught on something. So, to assuage these feelings, I started wrapping a hairband around my head and tying it at the back of my neck.

I made it through my first year of high school, wig in place, and I was over the moon mid-summer when my hair had finally grown to a length that I deemed sufficient to reveal to the world. I had bittersweet thoughts as I removed my wig for the last time. I was happy to see it go, but it had been a faithful friend, never once letting me down. Over ten months of almost daily wear and frequent washing had taken its toll. The wig looked pretty shabby, especially around the part where many strands had fallen out, leaving a noticeable bald spot.

As I bid my wig a fond farewell, my thoughts turned to life with short hair, something I hadn't experienced since Grade 1. Actually, that's only half true. In Grade 6 I had my long hair cut into a mullet—business in front, party in the back, baby! I shuddered when I thought about how much time it would take to grow my hair long again. However, on a positive note, I'd be starting Grade 10 with real hair;

no more worries about wigs falling off or the antics of evil butterflies.

A Fine Kettle of Fish

My hairdresser told me that after you lose it, hair can grow back very differently from what it was before—curlier, darker, lighter, even a completely different colour. I was quite blonde as a young child and, stereotypes aside, I thought it would be cool to be a blonde again. However, the only change was that my hair became finer. This wasn't a big problem because, although my hair was less thick than before, it had maintained its fullness. I figured that perhaps, unlike me, dramatic hair changes only happen to people who go completely bald.

I ended up growing my hair out longer than ever before, a few inches past my shoulders, for the next two years. But this was not the end of my hair nightmare. Enough with the tresses stresses for now.

CHAPTER THREE:
A PRECIPICE LOOMS

Shiny Metal Paper Towel Dispenser

Early January 1991. I was eighteen years old and in Grade 13. The first semester was over and final exams would be starting soon. Only one semester and one summer stood between, "Goodbye high school, hello new, exciting university life!" In the meantime, I was enjoying my senior year. I had a lot of friends and an active social life. I was even signed up for a dream school trip to Europe in the spring.

Turning nineteen was going to be pivotal for me. In a little over six months, I'd be off to university. I would be leaving home for the first time, taking care of myself and making more of my own decisions. Although it wasn't yet confirmed, my marks were high and I was certain I'd be accepted to my university and program of choice. I would spend at least my first year in residence on campus and meet a lot of new friends. I was both excited and nervous about what seemed like a 180° life change for a small-town girl.

That's when the fatigue set in again. I wasn't as wiped out as the first time, but I knew enough to take it seriously, especially because I could feel something in one of my lymph nodes. I shared the news with my parents, but I wasn't going to say anything to my brothers or close friends until there was confirmation. My dad had told me that when Ted heard of my diagnosis in Grade 8, it upset him so much that he failed one of his Grade 13 midterms.

I had built a good relationship with Shelburne Hospital lab staff through my frequent visits during my three-year maintenance protocol. But those days were long past, and when I walked into the lab this time, there was no friendly banter, only polite hellos and concerned looks. I'd gotten used to needles over the years, but I didn't usually watch while the nurse took my blood. This time I was watching, and maybe it was my altered state of mind, but I thought my blood had a kind of cloudy look.

As my parents and I met Dr. S after another round of blood tests, my focus shifted to the shiny metal paper towel dispenser above the sink as his voice grew dimmer. I had heard enough and I needed a distraction to take my mind off what I already knew was coming. Apparently, 93 per cent of all communication is non-verbal, and this proved to be true the previous day when I visited my family doctor. While his words said the diagnosis was not yet confirmed, his sad facial expression and grim tone said that it was—no question. But he was going to let the expert verbally confirm what he was non-verbally communicating.

As I stared at the paper towel dispenser, I tuned out talk of treatment, long hospital stays and survival statistics. My teenage mind and "glass half empty" predisposition turned to sad farewells to school, my friends, my social life, Europe and university in the fall. However, each of these farewells paled in comparison to the reality of losing my long, full hair—again! It was a 180° life change indeed, just not how I had planned.

My mind buzzed back and forth between sadness and hope. I heard two familiar words: chemotherapy and radiation. But there was also a new phrase: bone marrow transplant (BMT). Similar to leukemia, I had heard of BMTs—something about a donor's good blood replacing another person's bad blood—but that was it. Dr. S told us that I had to get back into remission before a BMT could even be considered.

OK, been there, done that.

I knew what I was facing this time, and my faith, family and friends would help me get through it again. Afterwards, I'd get the good blood transplanted inside me and then start building my life back to normal, like I did before. My fears waned a little more when Dr. S mentioned that there was no three-year maintenance protocol after a BMT, just blood tests and outpatient hospital visits for several months to check things out.

So my mind returned to my hair (typical teenager!). While I dreaded the thought of another wig, I figured that wigs would be even more realistic and designed to stay on better after five years. Also, my university peers wouldn't know me and I'd make sure they never figured out my secret.

That's when I was transported back into the fully woeful zone—*Would I even be able to go to university in the fall?* I was likely going to miss most or all of the next semester. My dad was a coordinator in the local school district and he would surely be able to arrange a way for me to complete my courses in time to attend university in the fall, right? I was on the cusp of entrance into the pleasant zone as I recalled how it was late March when I was diagnosed the first time around, but this time it was January. I'd have even more time to complete my treatment, transplant and courses. As for the BMT, it couldn't be any more difficult than what I'd already been though—kinda like a second step on the same level.

Step It Up

While it seemed like they were hours long, my thoughts only lasted a minute or so; they were fleeting. When I came back to reality after the last trip, another rude awakening awaited. The transplant itself would be relatively easy, similar to getting a blood transfusion, and I'd had lots of those. However, the step between getting into remission and getting the transplant was definitely not on the same level, not even close. The steps following the transplant would be on an even higher level—I was in for the fight of my teenage and early-adult life.

Things got even more terrifying as Dr. S spoke of why the pre- and post-BMT steps were so high, starting with finding a donor match. Unlike blood banks, there are no bone marrow banks with stem cells packed by type and ready to distribute when needed. If you're like me and have no clue as to what stem cells are, they're simply the building blocks of blood that are produced in the bone marrow. This is why BMTs are also referred to as stem cell transplants. The similarity between blood transplants and BMTs is the procedure itself—hooking the recipient's and the donor's extracted stem cells up to an IV and waiting for the beep indicating the procedure is completed. Blood type actually plays no role in donor matching, as the donor and recipient don't have to share the same blood type. Although, if it's not already the same, the recipient will take on the same blood type as the donor after the transplant.

A match is required between donor and recipient marker proteins, called human leukocyte antigens, or HLA. These HLA markers are present on almost all body cells, approximately two hundred per cell. Six specific HLA markers are tested during donor matching. Only six out of trillions of HLA markers need to match? Easy peasy lemon squeezy! So what's so terrifying? The HLA markers are unique per individual, making it rare to find an acceptable match. It was terrifying to hear Dr. S explain, as sternly as ever, that each sibling (same mother and father) had a whopping 25 per cent chance of matching. Each parent had a one in twenty thousand chance of matching. For everyone else, there was a one in forty thousand chance.

Armed with this uplifting news, it was time to switch my focus to getting back into remission. The process was pretty much a carbon copy of my 1986 experience: about a month of chemotherapy, radiation, painful procedures, trips to the pleasant and unpleasant zones of la-la land, barfing, the runs, etc., etc.

However, it wasn't all bad.

Family and friends visited often, I got a lot of cool presents, I adored my nurses and I went into remission quickly. Best of all, and to my utter astonishment, most of my long hair was still intact! On top of that, I could go back to school for about six weeks to give my body a break until Dr. S deemed me ready for the next step. However, when I gave it more thought, I began feeling much less keen on going back to school even though my hair was someway decent and I was at the top of the school, not the bottom.

High School Dropout

Sorry Mom and Dad, you'll be hearing this for the first time. School just wasn't where I wanted to be, and I decided to skip it whenever possible. I had justifications for my decisions, even though I knew deep down that they held little to no weight. Even though I would be back at school part way through the semester, I'd dropped one of my classes for health reasons. I also had a spare, so that left two courses, and I could find out what the homework was from friends when I skipped.

These, however, weren't my primary justifications. I was "that girl" again. Most people hadn't seen me for a while, and those who had, told me that rumours about me were back. Not that I was surprised—naïve teenagers know even less about BMTs than leukemia. My hair hadn't fallen out, but it was noticeably thinner, and I was just too darn proud.

I didn't skip every class. For the short time I was back at school, I'd say I attended more than half. When I didn't feel like attending, I would hang out with friends who were on their spares or sometimes just by myself. Shawn still lived on 2nd Avenue West. He had already graduated, but he was taking an extra year to work before going to university. When I didn't feel like being in the building at all, I'd walk straight to his house after the bus dropped me off (we had moved to rural Shelburne a few months after I started Grade 11) on days when I knew he wasn't working.

Another time, when I especially didn't want to be in the school building, I walked over to visit Shawn, not knowing if he was working or not. He was home, but it would only be a short visit because he had to head to work soon. I didn't feel like going back to school and it was way too early for Shawn to drive me home, so I reasoned it out. Cons: while I could take my time walking home, there's only so much time I can waste; plus, it's raining and I'm gonna get soaked. Pros: I remembered my mom saying that she was going out early in the afternoon, so she should be gone before I arrive. Also, I didn't need a key because I'd snuck unnoticed into the house many times through the basement window.

The pros won and I decided to walk the five miles home in the rain.

As I walked, I realized that I hadn't considered what to do if my mom arrived back home and it was too early for me to be home from school. My devious mind soon figured out a plan. I could hide out in my room until it was close to the time for me to be home. Then I could slip back outside via the basement window, keep low and scramble up the hill to the neighbour's property. I could get onto the road from there, then walk to our driveway and head up like I always did after the bus dropped me off.

However, when I got to the top of the hill between our house and the neighbour's house, I noticed that the car was still there—Crap! I was sure my mom would have left by now. I waited a while, but nothing—Crap! I needed another plan. I quickly ran down the side of the hill where I wouldn't be seen even if my mom came outside to the car, and knelt down. Staying low, I crept around the house to the basement window. I slid it open about an inch and leaned in close to listen if she was downstairs. I heard nothing. Then I opened the window wide and quickly wiggled through it, hid until she finally left and spent the rest of the day watching TV. Thankfully, I didn't have to carry out my devious plan, but I remember thinking how that was a lot of effort for little gain. Not to mention that spending all that time in the rain was pretty stupid as I was prone to infection due to my lowered immunity.

There are other school skipping experiences that stand out in my mind. One of the most memorable happened when one of my grandmas was visiting and she let me drive her car to school—a real treat because I hated the bus. As I approached the school, I made a quick right and headed to Orangeville, the big metropolis of Dufferin County. I wasn't sure what to do so I just drove around for a while. I didn't know anyone in Orangeville, but I didn't dare go to the mall or any other highly populated place because my dad worked at the Orangeville board office and I was afraid of running into him or someone he knew. The most exciting thing I did was order my favourite Filet-O-Fish, fries and root beer at the McDonald's drive-thru. I drove around a little more, then parked somewhere and rested for a while. Finally, I headed home, stopping to fill up the gas tank and arriving at the time I normally would if I had been at school.

Match Game

On March 4, 1991, I had to return to Sick Kids and talk with Dr. S about the next step. Although I wouldn't be leaving school yet, there was important business to take care of regarding finding me a bone marrow donor. A day was booked for my entire family to visit Sick Kids and have their blood taken and tested for matching.

I don't remember a lot about that day except ever so sweetly reminding my brothers how they were the patients who would have (what seemed like) gallons of blood taken. It would take a while before we would find out if I could move to the next step or be placed on the donor list. The latter option would be problematic as it can take months, even years (if ever), to find a donor. Even if a donor was found, non-familial donor tissue carries a greater risk of complications such as the recipient's immune system rejecting the donor's stem cells.

Autologous transplants, another option where a person's own healthy tissue is used when a donor isn't found in time, also carry a higher risk of these complications. Even a familial match, considered to be perfect, comes with risks as only identical twins have identical matches. Fun fact: 1986 was the last year before additional testing for viruses like AIDS and hepatitis were performed on the potential donor's blood. I suppose this fact wouldn't be so fun if I had tested positive when those who had donor blood-demanding procedures like BMTs pre-1987 were called a few years later to get tested.

March 6, 1991. My mom and dad were at work and my brothers were away at university, so I was home alone. The call was due any day, so my parents let me stay home from school. I was watching *General Hospital*, my favourite soap, so it must have been sometime between three and four o'clock. Robert had kidnapped Anna and tied her to a pole, when the phone rang. I turned down the TV, waited a few seconds, took a deep breath, then gingerly picked up the receiver.

"Hello?" I said weakly.

I could hear hootin' and hollerin' in the background as a shaky voice said, "Hi, is this the Murray residence?"

"Yes, it is."

"You have a match, your brother Mike is a perfect six out of six match and we're celebrating here at the hospital!" said the muffled voice of a nurse on the other end.

Staff would have a better understanding of the magnitude of these words than I would at the time. My nurses had told me that more often than not, they had to make calls sharing the opposite news. Dr. S's reaction helped me gain a better understanding as he rarely expressed his emotions. This time when we met, his face lit up like Canada Day fireworks when he congratulated me on beating some major odds. Even then, however, I thought of it as God's doing instead of beating odds.

After I hung up, I walked around the house with my hands in the prayer position, repeating the words, "Thank you God," over and over for I don't know how long until I remembered that I was supposed to call my dad as soon as I heard the news. Dad's voice was full of emotion as he praised God for His blessings. Mom expressed similar emotions and even told me later how confident I was that I'd get a match.

Risky Business

I'd made it through the first huge pre-BMT step, now on to the second. If you asked Dr S, he would summarize the procedure in his signature wigging-out-the-calmest-soul way: kill or cure. While his summation was dark, it was accurate. Before the transplant, your immune system must be completely wiped out to make room for the donor's stem cells. These cells travel to the bone marrow and start creating new healthy blood cells. Eventually, a whole new immune system develops. This is the ideal outcome to achieve a cure; however, sometimes when donor cells come across remaining healthy recipient cells that they don't recognize as part of their own, they can launch an attack, sometimes to the death.

In the 1980s, BMTs were high-risk procedures. Non-functioning immune systems produce fewer red blood cells and platelets, which causes anemia, at best. Much worse, there could be bleeding in the lungs, gastrointestinal tract, brain and other parts of the body. In addition to pneumonia, recipients were at a much higher risk of developing serious bacterial, viral, fungal and other infections. Graft failure was also serious, and it occurred when donor stem cells failed to take over the role of producing blood cells for the recipient's body. This might occur as a result of infection, recurrent disease or if the donated stem cell count was insufficient to cause engraftment. At the time, a writer from the Sick Kids magazine came to my hospital room asking for a comment on how it feels to be undergoing treatment in preparation for a BMT. I was so ill that I could hardly speak, but I clearly remember saying, "You forget what it's like to be well." It had taken about a month to get me back into remission, but now they'd completely wiped out my immune system in just a week with intense chemotherapy and radiation treatments.

By my third and final day of full-body radiation, I had to travel to a nearby hospital in an ambulance. I could barely function and I wasn't much better the previous two times when I travelled by taxi. Needless to say, the intense treatments meant I was extremely nauseated almost 24/7. Soon, I couldn't keep anything down, so I had to be tube-fed. My fluid intake was also increased via IV as I became severely dehydrated from all the puking and hot and runny spells. Would I ever feel well again?

Hope You Enjoy Your Stay

After my final radiation treatment, I was placed in what's called a positive pressure—or isolation—room. These rooms play a vital roll in successful BMT outcomes because they maintain a higher pressure inside the room than that of the surrounding environment. This allows air to leave without circulating back in, keeping germs, particles and other potential contaminants in the surrounding environment from entering the room. This room is closed off, and before entering, people must scrub their hands and put on a mask, gown, and head and feet covers in an adjacent room. As the recipient's blood counts start to rise, fewer personal protection equipment is needed; the mask is the last to go.

During my stay at the Healthy Air Inn, steps were taken to make my isolation period as tolerable as possible. I couldn't wait until I felt well enough to start using the Nintendo system and my favourite Mario Brothers game set up just for me (remember, this was 1991). However, those were the days when hospital room TVs were mounted inches away from the ceiling. When the day came that I felt well enough for a play date with Mario and Luigi, I turned on the Nintendo but soon realized that I could hardly see the screen. What was a girl to do? Stand up on the bed, of course! This did the trick. Seeing me in my hospital gown, standing on the bed and making strange movements as I manoeuvred the joystick gave staff and visitors a good laugh. This was a sign that I was recovering. They also put a stationary bike in my room to help strengthen my legs after so much time in bed.

It's Showtime

I'd be having the transplant two days after I entered the isolation room. Mike's stem cells would be extracted on the same day. Donors are admitted to the hospital the day before the harvesting procedure, and to add insult to injury, that day just happened to be Mike's twenty-first birthday.

Transplant day was relatively easy for me as there had been no harsh chemo or radiation treatments since I entered the isolation room. I was starting to discover what it was like to be well again. The nurse arrived to prep me for the procedure and hook me up to an IV. While I lay comfortably watching a rerun of *The Cosby Show*, Mike was in the recovery room after sedation from the bone marrow harvesting procedure started to wear off.

There are a couple of versions of how this procedure is done. The G-rated version says the donor goes under general anesthesia while a needle is inserted into the hipbone to withdraw stem cells from the bone marrow. If you want the X-rated version, it goes something like this: While the donor lays, highly sedated, on their stomach in an operating room, horse needles are plunged—not once, but multiple times—through the donor's skin and into the hipbones on both sides where one to two quarts of their stem cells are aspirated. True, the donor can't feel the actual procedure, but when they wake up in the recovery room after the sedation starts wearing off—*whammo!*—like someone is kicking them in both hips with steel-toed boots. Removing so many stem cells causes mild anemia, and the donor has to take iron pills for a while. Some require blood transfusions to get their blood counts up to a healthy level.

As my brother's healthy stem cells entered my body and began their dangerous quest to build me a new immune system, I remember receiving a phone call.

"Hello?"

"Hi, it's your Aunt C, what are you up to?"

"Nothing much, just having a BMT."

That's not what I actually said, but wouldn't that have been awesome if I did? I wonder what her response would have been? I just told her that I was doing well and she said that she and my uncle would visit me soon. The transplant was finished after about a half an hour and the race was on to the three gargantuan post-BMT steps.

The Waiting Game

Just like the BMT itself, the three post-BMT steps weren't big on pain but rather on an emotional level, which not only lasted longer but also felt worse at times—no help from Mr. Morphine this time! Waiting can cause amplified fear, anxiety and stress, especially when the results you're waiting for are life and death.

The first post-BMT step is called "engraftment," when healthy donor cells reach the recipient's bone marrow and start producing new cells. Void of an immune system, this is the stage when recipients are at high risk of developing serious bacterial infections and other risks like graft failure. Usually engraftment occurs ten to thirty days post-BMT. I don't recall how many days it took for my engraftment, but I do remember Dr. S telling me that I actually set a record for fewest number of days thanks to Mike's Grand Prix stem cells.

Once engraftment is achieved (determined via hipbone assaults), the chances of serious problems occurring progressively decrease. More assaults are a necessary evil to determine when blood cell counts have risen to the point where recipients have reached something called "step-down." If so, doctors, nurses, family and anyone else who enters the isolation room can start removing personal protection equipment. At the end of this stage, patients are often moved out of the isolation room and into a private room as they await entry into the final—and best—stage: discharge!

Unlike the three-year follow-up protocol following post-ALL remission, post-BMT protocol was three months of weekly check-ups to ensure there were no serious complications, that the cancer was under control and that the new bone marrow was functioning properly. Each visit started with blood tests, and after oncologists read the results, they determined things like whether or not patients needed more tests, more medication or even a blood transfusion. When the three months are over, the doctor decides on the frequency of follow-ups moving forward based on the patient's overall health.

Don't You Forget About Me

My first hospital release was on May 13, twenty-six days after the transplant. Restrictions on where I could go outside of the house and how many people I could be around lessened as my blood counts normalized.

On September 4, 1991, my blood counts were declared perfectly normal and all restrictions were lifted. However, while the first year post-BMT carries the highest risk of developing serious and life-threatening complications, you're never truly out of the woods 100 percent. Like many survivors, my memories of the first and second times around with The Big C faded as the years went by. After almost three decades in remission, I'd forgotten about one of the most common post-BMT complications: the development of new cancers.

CHAPTER FOUR:
GOD CHOOSES THE ZONK

New Diagnosis

Fast forward twenty-eight years to December 2018. It was the end of one of the best years of my life. I'd travelled to Florida with Mike, staying on the Universal Studios grounds and riding the super-scary rollercoasters that I love so much. In June, Mike and I joined our parents in London, England, for a twelve-night Baltic cruise vacation of a lifetime. In August, I was hired for a dream job as library accessibility coordinator and Accessibility for Ontarians with Disabilities Act (AODA) advisor at the University of Waterloo, my alma mater.

However, the year was going to end with an unpleasant surprise. Just before the Christmas holidays, I was in the shower and I thought I felt a small growth in my right breast. I suppose that almost thirty years free from The Big C left me in denial because I let it go. I checked it out again in February, and although the growth was still there, it didn't seem to be any bigger, so I let it go again. But by the end of March, not only was the growth bigger, I felt another small growth. You can't change the past, and woulda, coulda, shoulda is a recipe for a lifetime of regret. Still, I remain perplexed as to why, after all this, I waited another week to ask my mom, the RN, to check it out.

I made an appointment with my family doctor and got in almost immediately. After his examination, he told me that while more tests were needed to be certain, there was a good chance of malignancy. I'd been down this road decades before with my first family doctor, and this doctor's body language was no different; there wasn't a "good chance" of malignancy, The Big C was definitely back, just in a different part of my body.

When I think about my prayers as I went through test after test before the final diagnosis was revealed, they remind me of a game show in which God and I were the contestants but He had final say on the choices. First choice: curtain #1—benign tumours. OK God, the experts think the growths are malignant, but You can do miracles, so please choose it. Next! Second choice: curtain #2—early stage breast cancer. I sure wish You'd chosen the first curtain, but You know what's best, plus stages 1 and 2 are highly treatable and curable, so go for it. Next! Third choice: curtain #3—stage 3 breast cancer. I never thought You'd let things get this far, but God, You are all wise and I did read that this stage still holds hope for a cure. Hey, I'll even give up one or both of my breasts, just please, please, please choose this curtain. Next! Only one choice remaining: the small box, the zonk—stage 4 breast cancer.

When it looked like stage 3 was going to be the final diagnosis, the plan was for me to have a double mastectomy followed by outpatient chemotherapy. I wasn't looking forward to losing the girls, but they were never even on my list of things I couldn't live without. And chemotherapy, well, I was a pro. Like I said earlier, stage three still held hope of a cure, and I would beat the odds.

When I told my supervisors about my initial breast cancer diagnosis, they assured me that I could keep my job. My family doctor had told me that many women diagnosed with stage three breast cancer are able to return to work soon after a mastectomy. The number of regular hours I could work depended on how I responded to chemo; however, usually only a day or two post-treatment was required before returning. Then there was the hair issue, but honestly, at this point, losing my hair again was pretty far from my mind.

May 29, 2019. My final test results were in and my mom came with me to the appointment. After my family doctor confirmed my initial breast cancer diagnosis, he put me in the care of a young oncologist who worked in Orangeville. Before I actually heard the words "stage four," the doctor was spouting out a bunch of medical terms and phrases that left me confused as to what the actual diagnosis was. Plain English, please! The pit in my stomach grew to epic proportions when I finally heard the words and felt my mom's hand touch mine in a loving but fruitless effort to comfort me. I could barely speak, but I wasn't going to let my emotions get away from me, not yet anyway. In a daze, we left the office and my mom called my dad to pick us up. The short car ride home was silent, but the silence would soon be replaced by sobs as I sat down in one of the living room chairs and burst into tears.

Between sobs I questioned why God would give me a dream job after years of being turned down and then allow this to happen. What was the point? My parents let me cry, encouraging me to get it all out. When I calmed down, my dad put things into perspective in the composed, reasonable way that only he could. Our family has a strong faith, and he reminded me that God has a reason for allowing things like this to happen. He also reiterated how positivity is as effective as treatment, probably more. This helped me a lot, however, I really needed to be alone for a while. Despite my mom's protests, I drove back home to my apartment in Waterloo.

The next day I returned to work and revealed the news separately to my supervisors. It was hard to keep my cool, but they were great, giving me their full support and assuring me that I could take any time off that I needed, including a few days to process the big blow. I also told a co-worker with whom I was close. She had a lot of knowledge on accessibility legislation and other aspects of my job, so I knew I could count on her to fill in some gaps in my absence. I passed on the "emotional leave" because staying at home alone with little to occupy myself meant my mind would start straying to worst-case scenarios. Worse, I'd likely get on the internet (which I was warned against) and focus on the most gloom and doom articles.

No Cure ... But Treatment

My family doctor called me about a week later with an appointment to visit William Osler Hospital in Brampton to meet my new oncologist. Dr. J (I'll call her) would have a treatment plan ready for me along with more information about stage four breast cancer and time for questions.

The waiting room was standing room only and an absolute zoo. I had my suspicions that most of the people were family members or friends accompanying the patients. I was at the hospital for about six hours before I finally met with Dr. J. She was a pleasant person, upbeat and probably close to my age. Among her first words were those that have stayed with me to this day: "Stage four breast cancer isn't curable, but it's highly treatable." Hearing those words allowed me to breathe normally again. I knew about the incurable aspect of my diagnosis, but I didn't know about the availability of highly effective treatments. I later learned from another oncologist how effective treatments were progressively appearing on the market. This time, there was no need to transport myself to the woeful zone of la-la land to escape what I didn't want to hear.

The first step in my treatment plan was to have an oophorectomy. An oofa what now? For those of you interested in word origins, "oophore" is from the Greek "ophoros," meaning egg-bearing. "Ectomy" is from the Greek "ektome," meaning excision. Yep, my ovaries were going bye bye—or should I say, ovary. My specific diagnosis was "ER positive HER2 negative breast cancer," and hormone blocking therapy was the primary treatment. Most of the production of the female hormones estrogen and progesterone takes place in the ovaries, so it made sense that getting rid of the source was the first step.

Dr. J scheduled an appointment for me to meet the gynecologist who would be performing the oophorectomy. Thankfully, I could get the surgery done at the hospital in Orangeville where my parents lived instead of travelling to the Brampton zoo. When the doctor entered and sat down, I held my breath and nearly fell over—this dude was a total hottie! Not good. I didn't want a hot dude digging around "down there." I'd always had female gynecologists with whom I felt comfortable. Now I was double-whammied: a women's doctor who was not just a guy, but a guy with movie star looks. I knew he was a professional, but I struggled to get these thoughts out of my head and I probably sounded like a babbling idiot as I answered his questions. I finally cooled off, and by the end of the appointment it was clear that this dude knew his stuff and would be an ideal person to perform the surgery.

There are various ways a surgeon can remove an ovary, and in my case, a laparoscopic approach was used. This approach is considered to be minimally invasive with a smaller risk of infection and faster recovery for patients. Dr. Hottie told me that the surgery would take about an hour. I'd be under general anesthetic while he used a small camera to look inside of my abdomen and make small incisions on my skin to allow removal of my ovaries. That was the plan, but the surgery ended up lasting much longer. While one of my ovaries was quickly found and removed, a lot of time was spent searching for the other one. In the end, I only had the one ovary removed. Dr. Hottie's best explanation was that the other ovary was likely absorbed or destroyed due to the amount of toxic treatments I'd had over the years.

New Meds

The surgery went well, and although I was sore, I was back to work within a few days. When I went to see Dr. J to find out about the next step, she told me I'd be started on tamoxifen, which blocks the actions of estrogen. After several months, I would be switched to two other medications: one that lowers estrogen levels and another that interferes with the growth and spread of cancer cells in the body. Six months after that, I'd have a CT scan to see how the medications were working.

One of Dr. J's assistants then took me aside and explained how some of the medications weren't covered by insurance. The costs for these drugs weren't in the hundreds, rather the thousands, and that's per month. One drug was particularly expensive, $6000 for a monthly supply of twenty-one capsules. That's $285.71 per capsule—yikes! He then talked about a publicly-funded drug program and how it would cover the majority of my drug costs. What a blessing—sign me up!

After my second visit to see Dr. J in Brampton, she told me that she and several other oncologists take turns seeing patients at the oncology unit at Headwaters Health Care Centre in Orangeville. What a relief—no more crowded waiting rooms and long waits! The area that houses Headwater's oncology clinic is a relatively new build, and they did an amazing job with its design. All of the waiting areas are named after trees like Willow and Oak. Waiting and treatment areas are bright and painted in soft, calming colours. The furniture, especially in the treatment areas, is quite comfortable and the staff are wonderful.

I started with monthly visits to have my blood taken and see an oncologist, not necessarily Dr. J. Every third appointment I would receive medication through an IV drip. The Big C had travelled from my right breast to vertebrae in my lower back, so this medication would help to keep my bones as strong as possible as they were assaulted with toxic medications. I had a total of three CT scans. The first test showed that cancer was mostly undetectable, and the next two showed that there had been no changes—God is so good! My hospital visits were downgraded to every three months because Dr. J was so happy with my progress.

There are many potential risks and side effects that come along with my medications. You've seen the commercials where a drug's risks and side effects are communicated just before the end by the person who holds the world record for number of words spoken in five seconds. So, I'll just skip to a few of the risks. At the time of my treatment, I was told that risks included a decrease in bone mineral density, and lowered white blood cell counts. Lowered counts, however, can put users at risk of serious infections that can lead to death. Periodically I needed an OK from an oncologist who had checked my blood test results and found an appropriate number of white blood cells. If the counts were too low, I had to stop taking one of the drugs for a week or so and then return to have another blood test.

After I started taking the more expensive drug there were several challenges receiving it from my pharmacy. My drug company representative started investigating these issues and finally discovered that there was a lot of incorrect information on my file. When the representative called me with the good news that everything had been sorted out, she hadn't heard the most recent story of my pick-up attempt at my pharmacy. I told her how a young woman, clearly not a pharmacist, rang up the till after retrieving my prescription and said, "That's $6000."

Come again?

We gave each other the same *That can't be right* look, and she went to get a pharmacist. The issue was soon resolved, and I had a good laugh with both the young woman and the representative when I told her the story.

Hairy Again

I was blessed to avoid almost all of the potential side effects and risks associated with my medications. However, I couldn't avoid two of the most common (and not even remotely serious) side effects: hair thinning and loss. Almost exactly one year after my diagnosis, I decided that my hair had become inappropriate for viewing outside of a small group of approved people. As a result, I was back to wigs thirty-five years after the first time around.

This time, I only wanted to find something that matched my hair colour and short hairstyle as closely as possible.

Short hairstyles were all I'd known for over twenty years as they made my now fine and thin hair look less so. I'm not complaining as I'd been blessed with super-talented hairdressers who did wonders with the little they had to work with. But due to the treatments I'd be on for the rest of my life, wigs were my future. This reality wasn't all bleak, as it would mean that short hairstyles were no longer my only option. The long hair I always loved was back on the market—and no waiting!

My plan was to bid adieu to my first wig and find one that was shoulder-length or a little below to ease such a dramatic change. I also didn't want to go back to wig shopping at a store. So, I researched several online wig vendors and settled on the one with the best reviews. I wanted a chin-length wig with bangs that was close to my hair colour but not necessarily made out of human hair like the one I'd had in Grade 9. I was leaning towards a synthetic wig because the salesperson told me they were not only cheaper but often looked as real as human hair wigs. A few wigs that met my criteria caught my eye, and I ordered one.

Delivery was fast, but my heart sank as I discovered that although the wig was styled just like the online picture and looked real, it wasn't even close to my hair colour. My natural hair colour is medium to dark brown and this wig was more like a light honey brown. I wore it, but not for long. I thanked this wig as I packed it up with the last one and soon ordered another in the same style but two shades darker. Wig shades on this website got progressively darker by twos—the previous one was an 8, and I thought I'd go darker with a 4 this time because of how light the other one was. I was taking a chance of ending up with three wigs I wasn't going to wear, and when I first opened the box, I thought that this was going to be the case. For a second time I was seeing a wig that was great in every way but the colour. This time the wig was much darker than my natural colour. However, I decided to stick with it because when I tried it on, I thought the colour looked pretty good on me.

I liked the second chin-length wig and wore it for a few months, but despite infrequent wear, I felt that the texture was feeling rough. Also, I was constantly pushing strands away from my face and my positive thoughts about the colour were fading.

I went back to the website of my trusty wig vendor, and this time I clicked on the section displaying human-hair wigs. Wowza! They were definitely more expensive than the synthetic ones, but I kept browsing until I came upon a lovely shoulder-length, layered wig with bangs. I was doubly blessed because not only was this wig 60 per cent off, but I could order it in the colour that I now knew was closest to what God gave me. Just like Goldilocks, I'd tried too light (8) and too dark (4), so colour number 6 should be just right. And it was. Great colour, soft texture, and I could now wear a ponytail or braid and use hair clips, barrettes and other accessories that I hadn't used in decades.

I grew fonder of my fourth wig each time I wore it, which wasn't often. Due to the coronavirus, I was mostly at home so there was no need to take the time, minimal as it was, to style it. I purchased hats online before I began wig shopping, and I wore them when I was around family and close friends or when I was out for supplies or appointments. I'd never been a hat person, but I liked my hats and felt comfortable wearing them.

You may have heard of or seen those "chemo hats" often worn by women undergoing cancer treatments who have lost all or the majority of their hair. Thankfully, I could wear several different kinds of hats (my favourites are called newsboy caps) because I only needed to cover up the sparse areas at the crown of my head. Granted, my bangs were also sparse and stringy, but all of my hats had brims that I could pull down so only a few centimetres of my forehead showed.

Everything Old is New Again

Bangs have been very important for me since my bout with shingles several months after my BMT. While they weren't quite as sparse and stringy as they are now, they've helped to cover up several large scars that shingles left on my forehead. There were several other scars caused by The Big C that left unwanted changes to my appearance. There are times when I feel like a creature who has been ravaged by everything The Big C can throw at it over thirty-five years; it would make a great horror/slasher movie, no doubt. Ever heard of a Babadook? He's a towering, shadowy bogeyman with long, claw-like hands and a pale, frightening face. He hides in dark areas and haunts the protagonists in a 2014 Australian horror movie of the same name. Well, I'm a "BABUDEEP," the creature that comes alive in chapter five.

CHAPTER FIVE:
BA*BUD*EEP: BLEMISHED, UNIBROWED & DISTENDED

I can now make light of many of the more unpleasant experiences in my journey with The Big C because I have become more accepting of the unwanted body changes I've experienced. I have also found peace from the regrets I used to dwell on when I let my appearance-related pride stand in the way of seizing opportunities that would have been good for me. Sure, if it was up to me, I'd have aged normally (and gracefully), accepting the age-related changes that everyone experiences along the way. But my physical imperfections made me a much more humble, thoughtful and compassionate person.

The letters in the acronym BABUDEEP are in italics in each of the next three chapters. Italicized letters relate to temporary or permanent alterations to my appearance stemming from a particular medication, infection or disease that I have taken or acquired over my journey with The Big C. It's quite a ride that isn't for the faint of heart, so brace yourselves. If you thought the last three chapters were on the low side, these next three trump all lows, even the Dead Sea, which I understand is the lowest point on earth.

Dr. Jekyll

Prednisone is a drug that often instills fear and foreboding in past and present users due to its lovely side effects (she wrote sarcastically!). I liken this drug to Dr. Jekyll and Mr. Hyde—out to do good and evil. I'll call it Dr. P. It's a glucocorticoid that's particularly helpful for people with autoimmune diseases like asthma, rheumatoid arthritis and lupus. As Dr. Jekyll, it treats inflammation, acting like an adrenal gland by producing a hormone called cortisol. Cortisol can stop areas of inflammation by suppressing the immune system. Dr. P can stop multiple areas of inflammation as it doesn't target a specific cell or cell function.

This tic-tac from hell is so powerful that it doesn't just provide relief from severe pain, it can also save lives. In fact, before Dr. P and similar steroids came on the market, there was no treatment for people with autoimmune diseases who were experiencing serious symptoms. Before the 1950s, 80 per cent of those affected died two years after diagnosis. No wonder the scientists who discovered the benefits of steroids like Dr. P were awarded the Nobel Prize.

Like the conditions I mentioned above, people diagnosed with ALL are given Dr. P to reduce inflammation and suppress the body's immune response. Although it's not fully understood why, it can even treat short-term nausea caused by chemotherapy. Dr. P's signature move in fighting ALL is convincing unwanted white blood cells to commit suicide—maybe less of a Dr. Jekyll and more of a Mr. Hyde move, but in a good way.

Mr. Hyde

Now to the alter ego—the evil Mr. Hyde. Taken in regular doses, the side effects aren't too bad. They may include insomnia, ankle and foot swelling, muscle weakness, irritability and headaches. Most people don't experience all of the side effects, and they almost always go away once treatment is completed. But when Dr. P is prescribed to be taken in high doses over several days or weeks, "hideous" is probably the best adjective to describe what Mr. Hyde can unleash on you.

Where to start? Let's go in alphabetical order. The second "B" in BABUDEEP—"Blemished." Good skin does not run in my family's genes. Unfortunately, out of the five family members, I drew the short straw. I matured a lot faster than many of my peers, and you can actually see a tiny red zit on my chin in an enlarged Grade 2 school picture. I survived grades two through five OK, but when grades six and seven hit, my face was a deluxe pizza. Grade 8 showed much improvement, and it seemed like my complexion was on the way back to some semblance of normalcy—that is, until my first long-term relationship with Dr. P.

The correlation between steroids and acne isn't known exactly, but suffice it to say that Dr. P is responsible for the marriage of immune system receptors and bacteria that produces greasy, grimy, red-headed offspring. Worse, these offspring may take advantage of thinning skin, another possible result of long-term steroid use, and decide to take up permanent residence in the form of scars. Thankfully, I survived my high school and university years without a major pizza or crater face, but the latter would become an increasingly accurate description of my mug as the decades passed.

Next up, "Distended"—cool word, huh? It means "bloated." Now I could have used "bloated" instead, but I already had "Blemished" and another "B" in the acronym BABUDEEP. Plus, I was going for something that sounded like Babadook, and a third "B" wouldn't work.

But I digress.

Forget about the formal definition of distended; let me paint you a more basic picture: chipmunk cheeks. Steroids like Dr. P create high hormone levels that cause fat to deposit at the sides of the face. When fat deposits appear on the cheeks and neck, the result is what's called a "moon face" as the swelling makes the face look much rounder than usual. Thankfully, I didn't have a moon face, but I did look like I had about ten nuts stored in each cheek. My enormous cheeks also affected the appearance of my mouth. If you put one hand on each cheek and then squeeze tightly, you'll get an idea of how my mouth looked. Pucker up, buttercup!

Resisting the Devil

I sported the blemished and distended look on and off during my first and second bouts with ALL. The look was never good, but it didn't always keep me down. Let me give you one example.

Mike spent his third year at a university in Germany. My parents were planning to visit and tour around nearby countries, and I was available to join them if I wanted. However, I was taking regular doses of Dr. P and my face reflected it. *How do I travel Europe when I don't feel comfortable leaving the house?* Despite my multitude of doubts, I didn't let my appearance get in the way of seizing an opportunity, and I chipmunk-cheeked my way through Europe. I felt self-conscious, but I have no regrets.

I was also cheeky when it was time to renew my driver's license picture. I still have that old driver's license, but looking at it no longer makes me cringe. Rather, I smile when I think how brave I was to face (pun intended!) the world with that look.

Hairy & Hungry

Ready for more? How about "Unibrowed"? You'd think that finding out about a hair growth side effect would be a good thing. I'm losing my hair, Dr. P grows hair—in your face, Mr. Hyde!

No such luck.

I did indeed grow more hair—everywhere but where I wanted it. Maybe it would be different for a guy, but I looked like a combination of Elvis Presley and Groucho Marx. Sideburns, a moustache and a unibrow to complete the look. OK, I am exaggerating (not about the unibrow), but that's what it felt like. I won't go into detail on other areas of my body that experienced a similar fate, but I will give kudos to the person who invented the lady shaver. Oh yeah, not only does Dr. P not grow hair on your head, but it also contributes to hair loss in that area. Now that's insidiousness at its best.

Just in case you thought Mr. Hyde couldn't do any more damage, he had another evil trick up his sleeve. I wanted to add the "I" in the word "Insatiable" to my BABUDEEP acronym, but it also wouldn't fit, so I'll just tell you about it.

Dr. P can increase your appetite, and if you're taking a strong dose, like I often was, you can become ravenous.

To make things worse, food tasted better—even things I didn't like started tasting good and I could not get enough. I also ignored warnings that eating too much, especially the junky stuff, could cause me to gain a lot of weight. Imagine an appearance-focused teenage girl poo-pooing the potential of getting fat! I remember eating my full dinner and then begging anyone to order me a medium pepperoni and cheese pizza. I practically inhaled that and still felt hungry. I don't know how I managed to remain a reasonable weight. Perhaps my self-indulgence made up for the weight I had lost when treatments reduced my appetite—not to mention all the barfing and cases of the runs.

A blemished, unibrowed, distended, insatiable creature. Could it get any worse? You'll just have to find out in the next chapter—if you dare!

CHAPTER SIX:
BA*B*UDEE*P*: BLEMISHED PHANTOM

Voldemort, Meet Your Match

I've talked a lot about suppressed immune systems and how they can be helpful by stopping areas of inflammation and not helpful by making people more prone to diseases and infections. There is one infection so sinister, so spiteful, so sickening, that it makes Dr. P look as innocent as unicorns and rainbows. I wrote its name earlier, and I'll write it once more, but after that it will be referred to as "he who must not be named" (HWMNBN).

Shingles.

Although this isn't everyone's experience, as its severity depends on factors such as age, immune system strength and where it takes up residence, it was mine—in spades!

I was first introduced to it when I was a little girl. My mom used to get cold sores, and I'd giggle when she referred to them as "herpes." The term herpes was sometimes thrown around in my junior and elementary school classrooms and schoolyards. The target was often some poor kid who was singled out when a clique wanted revenge on them (usually a mean girl thing). At that age I thought it was a bad thing you can get from sex. But when I was an older teenager, I became a herpes scholar and learned the difference between herpes simplex (the cold sore kind), herpes genitalis (the sex kind) and herpes zoster (the HWMNBN kind).

Everyone who has had chickenpox has a chance of developing HWMNBN as the virus remains dormant in your system even after you've recovered. Children and teenagers rarely get HWMNBN as their immune systems are usually stronger than an adult's. That is, unless they've undergone cancer treatments or taken steroids like Dr. P that lower their immunity. The intense chemotherapy and radiation treatments I'd endured to wipe out my immune system prior to having a BMT created an ideal environment for HWMNBN—I'm talking Hollywood mansion. I'm sure this has changed, but before HWMNBN raided my body, I never really got a full explanation of what it can do to the recipient. Perhaps because I wouldn't be able to handle the gruesome details.

HWMNBN commonly manifests itself as blisters that wrap around either the right or left side of the torso in a single strip. The fact that it travels along nerve pathways accounts for the often extreme pain it causes. Pain occurs before the blisters appear and worsens after. Other pre-blister symptoms include numbness or tingling, sensitivity to touch, and fever. These symptoms are followed by a red rash, making it indisputable that HWMNBN is on the way. Until the blisters scab over, HWMNBN is contagious to anyone who isn't immune to chickenpox. However, chicken pox, not HWMNBN, is the infection caused by physical contact with blisters.

In my case, the blisters decided to take a different route, travelling along the nerves around my right eye, down my nose and up to my forehead. I can't express enough how thankful I am to have a mom who's an RN and can see the early signs. If left untreated for too long, HWMNBN in this area can cause painful eye infections that may result in vision loss. Extreme pain was the only symptom I recall prior to the blisters appearing. My family doctor diagnosed me right away, October 3, 1991, to be exact, and I was immediately taken to emergency where I was reintroduced to my old pal Mr. Morphine. Boy, was I glad to see him. It was bad enough when I was doubled over in pain on my bedroom floor, but now I was in agony. I soon drifted off into the pleasant side of la-la land, blissfully unaware of what I would wake up to see.

A Scarry Time

"Blemished," here we go again. Dr. P-induced acne is one thing; HWMNBN-induced scarring is a whole other. My cocktail of intense radiation, chemotherapy and prolonged steroid use were a scar's best friend. When a BMT is added to the mix, now you're BFFs. While thinning skin is a common side effect from cancer treatment and steroid use, it usually returns to its previous thickness once treatment is completed.

In my case, any breakout or other lesion (like HWMNBN blisters) became much more prone to scarring because my skin was no longer producing sufficient collagen and elastin healing agents. This does not paint a pretty picture in the initial stages. Warning, the following contains graphic material that may not be suitable for young or easily grossed-out readers. Please refrain from eating while reading.

When I woke up from my serene slumber, I still had some pain but it was under control. My memory is foggy, but my parents had to prepare me before I could look in the mirror. If I hadn't been sitting down, they would have told me to.

"You won't always look this way," Mom said as she held a mirror up to my face.

I instantly discovered why Jason wears a goalie mask in the *Friday the 13th* movies.

Clusters of blisters filled with fluid that would later pop and ooze covered and partially closed my right eye, ran down the middle of my nose and up to the middle of my forehead in a clump that was a little bigger than a gumball. They turned into scabs after about a week, but my right eye was an ooze fest for much longer—red, puffy, pussy, sore.

Once the scabs formed, the pain began to ease, but there was a new adversary ready to make my life even more miserable: itching. I'm not talking mosquito bite itching, nope. I'm talking so intense I'd have tie down my arms to stop scratching. I was given a cream to help relieve the itching, but this was like putting a band aid on a broken leg; it did nothing to help. I was warned that too much scratching would remove the scabs before the skin had time to heal and I'd get scars.

Scars, smars, I needed relief and I needed it now.

I ended up scratching off a lot of the scabs and I have the scars to prove it. I later learned that scratching or no scratching, I would have ended up with scars due to my thin, damaged skin.

Before I accepted the reality of HWMNBN-scarring for life, my dad told me about a man he knew who had HWMNBN in the same area and with the same severity. His scarring was almost invisible, and he was OK with me visiting him to see for myself. I was nervous about going, but my curiosity and hope spurred me on. After my parents and I settled down in his living room, he came over and had a close look at my face; anyone else wouldn't have gotten within twelve inches. He smiled as he told me that he looked very much the same at this stage and he was convinced that eventually my scars would also fade. My spirits lightened and it was a joyous ride home.

Enter Dr. S. Remember him? My stern, tell-it-like-it-is, joy-evaporates-as-he-enters-the- room oncologist? I had a follow-up appointment with him not long after the meeting and told him about the man's positive and encouraging words. As I spoke, Dr. S's expression turned hard. I appreciate his frankness now, but I was furious when he told me that there was little chance that my shingles scars would fade. The redness would go away and the scars would eventually become the same colour as my skin, but they would always be noticeable. I wouldn't talk to him after that, so my mom took over communications. I walked straight to a door leading to a stairwell and started to bawl.

"What does he know?" I sputtered. "He didn't see that man and his healing. He can't predict the future."

Mom comforted me.

"There's no way these scars are going to stay noticeable," I wailed.

She agreed that Dr. S. didn't know my future and assured me that it was all in God's hands.

Should I Stay or Should I Go?

Not long after most of the scabs and pain were gone, I had a dilemma to face (pun intended!). My Grade 13 graduation ceremony was looming and there was no health-related reason for me not to attend. But there were huge pride-related reasons for me to skip it. The pea-sized scab that remained on the tip of my nose might as well have been peach-sized. I looked like a pirate because I had to wear an eye patch on my right eye with a gauze pad underneath to absorb the ooze seeping out of it. My hair had grown to a sufficient length to expose it to the public, but my bangs weren't long enough to hide the glowing red shingles scars on my forehead. If those weren't valid reasons, I don't know what are. My parents wanted me to go, my friends wanted me to go, even Ted wanted me to go.

Like peeling an onion, I tearily pulled back the layers of pros and cons. You know the cons, but there were a few pros. I really wanted to see my friends and teachers again. I wanted them to see for themselves that I wasn't near death and that aside from my appearance, I was the same ole me. There was one appearance-related thing that I was proud of. Despite the fluctuations in my weight and all the time spent in bed before and after my BMT, several months had passed and my body was looking pretty bangin', if I do say so myself.

I finally decided to go, still dreading the thought. My body was gonna look even better in my new, custom-made Laura Ashley dress. Having my tall, handsome brother Ted by my side was going to be a big confidence-booster. He was home from teacher's college doing a placement at the high school. As a bonus, my dad, who was now assistant superintendent for the school district, would be handing out the diplomas.

When God closes a door, He opens a window! I made it through the inevitable stares and whispers as we walked down the hallways and into the auditorium. My discomfort waned as I was hit with a barrage of hugs, kind words and praise for my courage and accomplishments. Again, another opportunity I didn't allow my appearance-related pride to lose.

Kids Say the Darndest Things

A few months later, my grandma on my dad's side passed away. A big family gathering where she and my dad's youngest brother and family lived had been planned months before for that same day. My family was already there, and I was on the way with my dad's middle brother and family with whom I'd been visiting over the past few days. There's never a good circumstance for someone's passing, but having all of the immediate family together at the time really helps.

My grandma had nine grandchildren all within nine years of each other. That was, until the surprise appearance of another grandchild six years after his older brother was born. He was about eight years old at the time, and as we all gathered in my grandma's apartment after the funeral, he pointed at my face and announced to everyone that I looked like the Phantom of the Opera. My dad's side of the family has the humour gene, and instead of chastising my young cousin for his inappropriate words, we all roared in laughter. Hence, the letter "P" for "Phantom" in the BABUDEEP acronym.

CHAPTER SEVEN:
*BA*BUD*EE*P: BARBIE-ARMED & ENFLAMED-EYED

Seeing Myself from a Different Angle

Barbie-Armed? Explanation please. The term "Barbie" is a lot like the term "Kleenex." They're specific brand names and proper nouns that have become common nouns used to refer to their counterparts. I had one actual Barbie and other Barbie-esque dolls with the brand names "Sindy" and "Darci." I even had a doll with the brand name "Suntan Tuesday Taylor." Not only would she get a tan when you put her in the sun, you could twist her head around 180° to change her from a blonde into a brunette and vice versa.

My Barbie was "Bride Barbie," and she wore a lacy wedding gown and veil, stilettos and had an enormous diamond engagement ring wedged into a drilled hole in her left hand (twisting heads, drilled holes in the hands—these must have been some macabre manufacturers). I could bend Barbie in half and bend her legs into a side split, but I could not bend her arms straight as they were at a permanent 90° angle. This wasn't so bad, as it allowed me to pose her in several groovy ways: holding her hips in anger when Darci made fun of her; placing one arm on her hips and the other demurely touching her cheek to flirt with Ken; or respectfully doffing her hat when G.I. Joe passed by.

So how does "Barbie-Armed" fit into the BABUDEEP acronym? Let's talk about graft-versus-host disease (GvHD), which I'll call the "Gang." At the time, there wasn't a lot known about it, certainly not compared to today. The "graft" is the donated bone marrow and the "host" is the recipient. Recall that only identical twins have identical matches. Although Mike's bone marrow matched the six criteria required to consider it a perfect match, he and I were not twins. Don't get me wrong, I've been ALL-free since 1991 and that's a huge blessing. However, my healing didn't come without consequences.

When the Gang attacks your connective tissues and joints, it can affect the tendons that connect muscle to the bone. When tendons become inflamed, they can shorten or contract muscles. This is what happened to me, and I can no longer fully straighten my arms. When I put every ounce of effort I have into straightening them, I can only get to about 120°. Not exactly like Barbie's 90° angle but still noticeable. I have to laugh to myself when people say to me, "You're tall, can you reach that for me?"

"I wish I could help," I say, holding my arms out, "but my arms won't let me."

Arm restrictions aren't the only thing that affect my reach. The range of motion in my shoulders is restricted to the point where I can't raise my arms above my head. My restricted heel-to-toe motion throws off my gait by forcing me to lift my legs higher to permit my feet to clear the ground and avoid tripping myself. Basically, the Gang caused my feet to drop, leaving me with little dorsiflexion (moving my feet and toes upward). The name for this condition is "steppage gait" or "high stepping." Over the years, young kids and residents at the long-term care facility where I used to work have innocently asked me, "Why are you marching?" This used to bug me, but now I just laugh and say something like, "I march because I always wanted to be a soldier!" Or, "I march because I'm happy!" Yet another name describing how I walk is "equine gait," something you can look up on YouTube; basically it shows a horse walking.

Actually, my tendons are restricted to some degree in all areas of my body, including my neck, back and hands. The muscle atrophy throughout my body has reached the point where if I were to sit or lie on the floor, I wouldn't be able to get up without assistance. High stairs and low chairs are not my friends, but railings and arm rests are my besties, and I always breathe a sigh of relief when we meet.

In all my workplaces, I've campaigned to remove physical access barriers inside and outside of public spaces. The costs aren't extravagant when plans for new builds include designs for equal access to both the outside and inside areas. In fact, the Ontario Building Code has added new requirements related to barrier-free paths of travel, adaptable seating and power door operators—and this is just the beginning. OK, I'm stepping off my OBC height-approved soapbox now to continue with more of the Gang's tomfoolery.

Renting to Own

Here I go again with the segues. Speaking of horses, I might have just put the horse before the cart, so I'll go back to how the Gang manifests itself.

An invasion from the Gang can actually have one positive effect due to something called the "graft-versus-cancer cell effect." During the transplant, the new stem cells seek to recognize and destroy any remaining cancer cells in the body. Aside from that, I have no other positive words to offer this posse of predators. In addition to the more acute impacts, there can also be milder attacks when the Gang initiates a fight with fisticuffs—fewer casualties, but still unwanted damage. Not long after I completed my jail sentence, a pinpoint rash appeared underneath the top layer of my skin. Thankfully, this rash wasn't itchy, but it was relatively widespread. I also got sores on my lips and inside my mouth. My eyes started to get watery, and in addition to the redness from HWMNBN, they looked pretty bad. Dr. S let me know that the effects could move from acute to chronic—when the Gang starts a knife fight with a much more serious outcome.

And move they did—in like a lamb, out like a lion. While Mike's stem cells were doing their job recognizing and killing any remaining cancer cells and building new, healthy blood cells, they encountered some of my remaining healthy cells that they didn't recognize and thought, "Whazzup?" The scenario might have played out something like this:

"This is the Gang's territory now and these dudes are trying to take over. We're not gonna let them get away with this—time to start a rumble!"

As I understand it, there isn't a concrete explanation as to why the graft rejects the host. Common explanations include donor cells not adequately matching the host's cells, and opposite sex donors putting the recipient at a higher risk of an invasion.

In both its acute and chronic forms, the Gang can "burn out" after several months or years. Dr. S mentioned this just before telling me that the chronic form can last a lifetime.

According to my editorialized version of his explanation, few areas of the body are immune to attacks, whether from fisticuffs, knives or even guns. After Mike's stem cells wiped out my enemy cells, they sent a message out to Gang members located in other territories, alerting them that they may also have to launch attacks in their hoods. I've only written about assaults from the Gang that continue to affect me, but in its acute form, it most commonly attacks the skin, bowel, stomach and liver. In its chronic form, it can also wage war on the lungs. I liken the Gang's residence within the body to either "renting" or "renting to own." Despite my numerous efforts, the landlord was unable to convince my rowdy tenants to move out, so it seems they are here to stay.

Memorable Trips

When I fall, I fall hard because my arm muscles are no longer strong enough to brace myself. This often causes bystanders to think that I fainted (I know this because I've heard them voice it). Thankfully, I can usually turn my body around in time to avoid a face plant.

One of my epic falls occurred when I was visiting Mike for the weekend and he wanted me to help him pick out some office duds at a busy clothing store. On the way out, I tripped myself up on the smooth, shiny floor and fell. I felt so bad for him as he struggled to follow my inadequate instructions to get me back up on my feet, but he has since mastered the technique.

I've had several other notable falls. One time I wasn't able to turn myself around as I fell getting out of the car, and I hit my forehead on a huge rock and required stitches. Another time, my dad and I were visiting Ted, and it was pitch-black outside when we left. My dad was just behind me when I fell, so he tripped over me, landing on my knees and lower legs. I was a little sore when I went to bed, but I soon awoke to pain that was so extreme and debilitating that I couldn't get out of my bed to get relief. Unfortunately, my room was in the basement and my parents were asleep in their room upstairs. My yells for help were too weak, so I turned up my radio full blast. This worked, and my parents came rushing down to my aid. I got some relief from an ice pack and Extra Strength Tylenol, but I really could have used a visit from Mr. Morphine that night.

Unless I fall forwards because I didn't get myself turned around in time, my head snaps back and hits hard on the surface due to my weakened neck muscles. In addition to headaches, my neck is often quite sore for a while after a fall. When I fall on a hard surface, the sound of my head hitting the floor is quite loud, like dropping a watermelon. Thankfully, my head hasn't yet exploded like a watermelon, but blood is so close to the scalp that if I hit it hard enough, it gets messy. If the wound is deep, I have to go to emergency and get it stitched up.

In my first year of university, I was in one of the older buildings where all of the interior doors are made of solid wood. As I was entering a washroom, I used my shoulder to help push open the door while another person pulled the door open from inside. Despite trying to stabilize myself with jetes and pirouettes that would make a ballerina jealous, I went splat. There were several other girls in the washroom at the time, and one of them started screaming when she saw blood gushing out of my head. I assured everyone that I was fine (physically, that is) and someone called the university health department.

My anxiety wasn't related to having to be helped up, rather, I was embarrassed to be lying in a pool of blood while the person blocking the door to keep others out yelled, "There's an injured person in here and there's blood everywhere!" Thanks so much for that, sister.

However, a Good Samaritan kindly stayed by my side until the cavalry arrived even though she would miss classes. She went the extra mile when the doctor told me that he'd have to cut off a fair amount of bloody, matted hair so he could see better, and she offered to de-matte the wound area. As she gently sponged away the blood with warm water, sparing my hair, I thought to myself, *Who does this?* Here I am focused on my stupid pride while this saint is sacrificing her time to help a total stranger. Humbling indeed!

I eventually had surgical procedures, called "tendon transfers," in areas below each ankle to help normalize my heel-to-toe movement and minimize the falling. My surgeon made a one-and-half-inch incision vertically below my inner ankle (apparently, there are muscles to spare down there), and after he found a working muscle, he cut it, attached it to a non-working muscle and then stitched me up. I had to wear a walking cast for several weeks after that, and then it was weeks of intense physiotherapy to normalize my gait. It was still off, but I rarely tripped myself up after that. When I did, it was usually because I tripped over something or I was wearing shoes with soles that were non-slip—my shoes stopped while the rest of me kept going.

Don't It Make My Hazel Eyes Red

Earlier I mentioned that the eyes were another area that the Gang, especially in its chronic form, may seriously attack. Vision wasn't a problem until I had to get glasses in my late forties. I had, however, developed teeny tiny cataracts from the full-body, intense radiation. In one of the rare times Dr. S delivered positive news, he said that my cataracts wouldn't likely become a problem and require surgery to remove them until I was much older. To date, my cataracts remain on the smaller side, so "much older" must have meant over fifty.

The radiation also wiped out my tear ducts, and this was exacerbated by attacks from the Gang. I already had other eye issues, like my inability to cry tears. My eyes get red but no tears fall because there's nothing to produce them. Strangely, this mystery, called dry eye syndrome, also made my eyes watery, but it wasn't the kind of moisture that soothes the eyes; more of a cloudy film that blurred my vision. So I had both dry and watery eyes. Dryness wasn't the only issue as, with no tears to flush it out, there was a lot of mucus build-up. Sometimes I'd wake up with my eyes sealed shut by dried mucus (maybe I should have issued the warning before I wrote that). My eyes also felt gritty and became very light-sensitive.

I remember sore, red eyes being a particularly big issue in the late nineties when I was earning a post-graduate certificate at a Toronto college. My dad would call to see how I was doing and I'd say, "I'm riding the red-eye again." This wasn't a ride I took every day, just most days. Sometimes the ride was a more peachy/pink colour or limited to the corners of my eyes. Every once in a while I caught a break and rode the clear-eye. On those days, I felt confident enough to actually look someone in the eyes. I did have over-the-counter eye drops that helped a little, and I tried to apply them as often as I could, but I prayed that something more effective would come my way.

My prayers were answered the day I was referred to an ophthalmologist (I'll call him Dr A) at another Toronto hospital. Like so many of my doctors, Dr. A was a unique person. He was a small but mighty man and very intelligent—a pioneer in his field. He also liked to be hugged when he "done good," which was a little awkward because I'm not a hugger. It's not surprising that my quest to conquer the evil enflamed eyes took flight after my first visit all thanks to something called "punctal plugs." "Puncta" are the tiny openings that drain tears from your eyes. For someone who can't produce natural tears, any fluid draining in the eye is detrimental. Enter the punctal plug, a silicone device about the size of a grain of rice that's inserted in the tear ducts to keep the eye surface moist and comfortable. Artificial teardrops were a close second to natural tears, and when I applied them, the plugs would keep any moisture from draining out of my eye unless I blinked it all away. Even then, some natural moisture produced by other bodily functions would remain.

What a God-send! Within days, my eyes were so much better, and I was riding the clear-eye most of the time. About two years later, I heard the whistle of an even clearer-eye train. My eyes were mostly clear, but some redness and a gritty feeling lingered. On a follow-up visit, Dr. A introduced me to a young intern ophthalmologist from Ukraine. She had been part of a team that developed a new form of eye drop called "autologous serum eye drops." These drops are a combination of the patient's blood plasma and artificial teardrops. What seems like a million vials of blood are drawn and then placed in a centrifuge to remove the plasma before finally being mixed with artificial drops. Plasma contains several components, such as vitamin A, that are present in natural tears and, as we all know, there's nothin' like the real thing, baby. It didn't take weeks or days or even hours—almost immediately after the drops were inserted, I could see and feel a difference. Even though I'm not a hugger, I wrapped that intern and Dr. A in an especially warm embrace.

No Help Wanted

The serum eye drops were one of many "assistive devices" that helped me overcome medical and physical barriers caused by the Gang. My limited range of motion and weakened muscles made it impossible to put my socks on by myself because I couldn't even bend down and touch my feet. However, an occupational therapist introduced me to a device that helps me do so, lickety-split. It's called a "reacher," and it made it easy to pick up items off the floor (even small, flat items like coins) and get things down from high shelves. An extra-long handled shoehorn (you can buy them at Walmart) offered me a way to get my shoes on by myself, and it doubled as an assist for clothing myself from the waist down. I simply hooked the shoehorn onto a belt loop or other area where it could get a good grip, and lifted it up off the floor until I could reach it with my hands and pull it on.

    I don't like asking for help, and I've become skilled at devising ways to overcome barriers when I have no assistive devices to help me. There have been several times when contents that were jammed into my mailbox came flying out onto the floor as soon as I opened it. When there was no one around, I would pick up the nearby garbage bin, lay it on the floor on its side, use my foot to sweep the contents inside, then pick up the bin, turn it right side up and retrieve my mail. I've gotten really slick at that trick. When I can't figure out a way to pick something up after I've dropped it and there are other people around, I have to swallow my pride and ask for help. Mind you, I don't swallow all of my pride as when I ask for help, I'll say something like, "I have a really bad back," or, "I'm having back problems," or, "I recently injured my back." Pathetic, I know.

So there you have it—BABUDEEP fully explained: Barbie-Armed, Unibrowed, Distended, Enflamed-Eyed Phantom, and—oh yes—hairy yet balding, with an insatiable appetite. A gruesome love triangle among Dr. P, HWMNBN and the Gang. Kudos to all the courageous readers who decided not to skip this chapter. Enough of these lows, it's time for an homage to each of those earth angels, also known as caregivers, who have devotedly and selflessly been there for me through every step of my journey with The Big C.

CHAPTER EIGHT:
KUDOS TO CAREGIVERS

A Caregiver by Any Other Name Would Care the Same

When I Googled the word "caregiver," almost every primary definition used the words "physician" and "nurse" in reference to the caregiver, and "person" or "patient" in reference to the "caregiven." These results made perfect sense, as they're likely what most people think about when they hear the word. I certainly did, and that's how I started planning this chapter.

I made a list of all of the "medical" caregivers I've encountered during my journey with The Big C, noting the memorable ways they provided care to me. However, my perspective changed when an online dictionary broadened the definition to "A person who provides direct care," and included children, elderly people and people with chronic illnesses amongst the caregiven. These are only some of many other possibilities.

Both caregiver and caregiven roles occur from the beginning to the end of our lives. Yes, even when we're babies. While it's not a conscious effort, think about all the joy babies bring to their parents and families. Toddlers become caregivers when they're tasked with taking care of and putting away their toys. Most parents put their children in charge of keeping their rooms clean and other chores like setting the table or mowing the lawn. If you had younger siblings, it's likely that your parents also put you in charge of them every so often. If you've ever had a pet, you're a caregiver because you're responsible for another life.

On the flipside, like babies, those you take care of often take care of you, meeting your emotional needs. Pets are a great example. Unconditional love is one of God's greatest blessings, and that's what most pets provide for their owners. It may not be on the same level, but pet therapy dogs are trained to "love-up" perfect strangers to offer them a welcome break from the problems and challenges of life. I worked for over eight years as the programs director at a long-term care home. When animals were brought in for visits, it was so heart-warming to see residents light up. As the residents stroked the animal's fur, they would often start reminiscing about "the good ole days" and their favourite pets. Many of the residents with advanced dementia who spent a lot of the day just sitting and staring blankly came to life when a dog rested its head on their laps.

As Strong as My Weakest Links

I don't mean to pop this positive bubble, and I'm definitely not taking a shot at caregivers, but sometimes being the caregiven can be a real drag. For those like me who grew up physically strong and then lost a lot of that strength and were forced to rely more on others, accepting help is particularly difficult. Another one of my fearless but stupid stunts was showing off by riding my bike with my arms in the air and both feet on the handlebars. When I inevitably wiped out, my front wheel was facing the opposite way, and my multiple cuts and scrapes left me dreading having to face my mom. The damage likely would have been worse if I wasn't so physically strong. My mom did force me to eat spinach, but in addition to good genes, I think my uber-active childhood accounted for my strong bod.

My mom sometimes remarked about how much she loved the chubby arms and legs I had as a baby and toddler. I wasn't overweight, I just had big bones and a lot of muscle. As I grew older, I would describe my body as "solid"—again, because of my bones and muscles. When help was needed, I was usually given the "heavy" jobs: lifting or moving something, or even climbing. I remember when I used to babysit three little girls who lived beside us. One night, when it was time for bed, they demanded that I carry them up the stairs together. So, with one on my back, one on my shoulders and one in my arms, I stumbled up the staircase to their room. It wasn't an easy climb, but I made it.

My strong bones created a big problem for an intern at Sick Kids one day when he was poking me with a needle to extract a sample from one hipbone. After he tried and failed a few times to get the needle through the bone, a more experienced doctor stepped in, remarking harshly to the intern that I'd had enough. However, even the expert wasn't successful the first time.

My physical strength is matched by my strong personality. I'm stubborn and strong-willed, which led to a lot of fights with my parents, brothers and friends when I was a teenager. I wanted my way, even at the risk of punishment, which was the result when I was defiant to my parents. As I've mentioned before, I've never liked asking for help, but I could sure give it, wanted or not. I suppose it was more like I thought my way was the best way to get things done, and I rarely paid attention to what anyone else had to say. If you were to look at several of my junior school report cards, you'd see something like, "She is a good student but can be very bossy at times." Also, like the cliché states, I could dish it out, but I couldn't take it. When you think you have all the answers, why do you need help from anyone else? Similarly, the results are often detrimental when the caregiven won't accept—or even consider—the help offered by a caregiver.

You've read about my CN Tower-sized pride and how I still balk at offers for help, which includes advice. There are hundreds of examples, but I recall two separate times when I didn't follow expert advice and paid the price. I love animals, and my parents accommodated this love by allowing me to have multiple pets when I was growing up. However, one pet I was not allowed to own was a cat due to my mom's severe allergies. When I was about six years old, my mom brought me with her to visit a friend. While they talked, I saw an opportunity to fill in the cat gap in my young life when I spotted one underneath a table. I was warned not to touch the cat, but I was determined to get that cat in my arms. When my desperate, "Here kitty, kitty, kitty..." pleas were ignored, I got a hold of its tail and yanked it towards me. The cat justifiably responded by scratching up my face pretty good, and one of the scratches on my left cheek was deep enough to require stitches. After he stitched me up, the doctor warned me not to be active for a few days to keep the stitches intact. I don't recall, but it was probably a day or two later when I got into a physical fight with my brother Ted over what TV show to watch. Sure enough, the stitches opened.

I detailed the horrors of the dreaded lumbar puncture (Lp) procedure earlier, but what I didn't tell you about is how there could be trouble if you don't follow the doctor's post-Lp instructions. I was supposed to lie flat on my back for at least an hour after the procedure, drink lots of water to rehydrate, and avoid vigorous activity for a day or two. The consequence of ignoring these orders can be something called a post-dural puncture headache (PDPH). The length and severity of PDPHs varies, but in my case, after about an hour on my feet, a headache would start and worsen until I laid flat on my back. If I waited too long, I would puke, making myself even more dehydrated.

I usually followed Dr. S's orders, but one of the times I didn't was especially disastrous. It was summer, and I was going on vacation with my parents and Mike a few days after having an Lp. I didn't remain flat on my back for the required time, nor did I avoid vigorous activity, so... whoomph, there it is! Thankfully, my dad had rented a Winnebago, so I could lie down on one of the beds while we travelled, but it was no fun having to do this for half the vacation.

Worse, one day I was pretty sure that the PDPHs had subsided, so Mike and I visited a nearby theme park where I could ride my beloved roller coasters. I was able to remain on my feet much longer than before, but the headaches still came several times, and I had to drag my poor brother to a bench or grassy place where I could lie down flat. At least one time I didn't make it and puked on my shoes.

Explain Yourself

So what's the point of my several-page rambles? To highlight the huge role caregivers play in helping us live our lives to the fullest potential and emphasize how we should at least consider their offers of service and advice. I'm not saying caregivers are always right, that you shouldn't get a second opinion or that you shouldn't do more research on what they're offering. I just mean that, in my experience, it was beneficial to sometimes accept offers of help, especially when the decision was pride-related. It may just be that they're doing their job, and the goal is the same: A true caregiver is looking out for you and your best interests even when it turns out that there's a better course of action. There are always exceptions, of course, but being suspicious of everyone gets you nowhere. That being said, my parents and I both accepted and turned down help from several brilliant caregivers who had my best interests in mind. The rest of this chapter focuses mostly on these earth angels, with an example of a questionable offer thrown in.

Above & Beyond

Let's start with the medical caregivers. You've read a lot about Dr. S and what a unique individual he is. He had a teddy bear heart inside his rough exterior, and the few times he opened up his heart to me and my mom were truly touching. Sometimes Dr. S's caring revealed itself through a second-hand source.

While I was in the hospital recovering from my BMT, Dr. S's assistant nurse told me and my parents that most doctors check on their patients' progress by either calling to have files read to them or making a quick stop to check out the files in person. In-person visits with their patients were only frequent when there was a problem. Dr. S frequently visited me in my room. Other days, he would greet me with a wave and warm smile (as warm as he could muster, anyway) outside my hospital room window. The nurse said that he mostly checked my file in person, which is when I likely received the window greetings.

The nurse also told us about how Dr. S had to jump through hoops to have my BMT done at the children's hospital instead of an "adult" hospital. Although cancer patients were sometimes transferred to the nearby cancer hospital sooner, eighteen was the cut-off age and I was turning nineteen two months before my scheduled BMT. Not only would I have been without my trusted, beloved Dr. S, but also my current hospital rolled out the red carpet for its patients and their families, attending to their every need (remember the Nintendo and stationary bike?). I didn't end up getting dumped into a big-girl hospital until well after I turned twenty. At that point I was fine to make the switch as I was feeling like a whale amongst the krill.

I've talked about my first family doctor (I'll call him Dr. H), but I haven't gone into detail regarding his unique character. My dad knew him best, and he referred to him as an "odd duck" (in a good way). He was also a brilliant diagnostician with a wide array of interests. I remember how he would talk (and talk and talk ...) to my dad, also a man of many interests, when Dad accompanied me to my appointments. I always loved hearing Dr. H's strong Irish accent and watching him as he mumbled indecipherable words into his Dictaphone (a tool my dad said he was addicted to). Dr. H. was fond of me, and he was bound and determined to get me where I needed to be when time was of the essence. I don't recall when or why, but apparently, he even came to our house in Shelburne (he lived in Orangeville) one day on his own time to take care of me.

I think I was in my late twenties or early thirties when Dr. H moved to the States. I was sad to see him go, however, following the usual doctor-related pattern of my life, our new family doctor (I'll call him Dr. D) was yet another blessing. Dr. D and my family attended the same church, and he had our full respect and admiration long before he became our doctor. He was the one who confirmed my initial breast cancer diagnosis, and he was my compass as I navigated through this scary and sometimes confusing journey. After he revealed the diagnosis, he pointed to a keychain attached to my car keys. The keychain was inscribed with the Bible verse, "I can do all things through Christ who strengthens me." (Philippians 4:18) He reminded me that I wasn't alone in my fight against this new version of The Big C. I still hold this verse in my heart and bring it to mind when the fears and doubts start.

I would be totally remiss if I didn't write about the multiple nurses and assistants whose caring was just as important and effective as any of my doctors. Nurses are so often the ones who get stuck with the dirty work: emptying bedpans, cleaning up the runs, performing sponge baths ... and the list of nasty tasks goes on and on.

I became close with one nurse who was wonderfully zany. She always made me laugh and lightened up tense situations. I remember one time when I wasn't allowed to get out of my hospital bed and had to use a bedpan. My bladder was about to explode, so she brought me a bedpan and left to give me some privacy. I ended up filling up the bedpan to almost overflowing, and when she returned to remove it, a good amount of #1 splashed onto her arms. I felt awful and super embarrassed, but she faked a look of utter disgust and hilariously admonished me for my cruel trick that was purposefully done just to spite her.

I also built relationships with several young nurses. When you're a patient in your late teens, some of the nurses are more like your peers because they're not much older than you. I often found it easier to open-up to a young nurse about certain health-related things that were difficult to share with my parents, let alone someone like

Dr. S. Even better, I really missed seeing and talking with my friends (no cell phones back then; only snail mail and visits every so often), and it was so helpful for my psyche when I could talk with these nurses about things young people are into, like the latest music and movies, instead of the usual medical mumbo jumbo.

A Doctor by Any Other Specialty ...

"Doctor" and "nurse" are words commonly associated with the term "caregiver," but naturopaths were a great help to me as well. It's such a shame that doctors and naturopaths often can't seem to work together in North America like it seems they do—often in the same clinic—in Europe. I've been seeing naturopaths for years, and their wisdom often complements that of my myriad of doctors. The approach may be different—doctors healing patients versus patients healing themselves—but they're not mutually exclusive.

Speaking of approach, I found the focus my naturopaths put on poo a little off-putting at first. Every time I visited my first naturopath, he would ask me about the colour of my poo—"Does it look like my desk? That bookcase over there? How about this picture frame?" My other naturopath was more focused on my #2 frequency—"Once a day, twice a day? How about four times a day like me?" They went on to explain that stool colour can reveal whether or not you're eating the right foods or if there's a sufficient amount of bile present to digest fats. In terms of poo frequency, it can also be an indicator of one's health, with one to three times per day as the norm. I wonder how often we think of having a poo exam?

All jokes aside, my second naturopath introduced me to what's called a "vibe plate" after I was diagnosed with osteoporosis. It is essentially a vibrating platform you stand on that forces many muscle groups to work to stabilize you. This product was originally designed in Russia to promote bone density for astronauts in space, and that was also the goal for me (even though I'm not an astronaut—but wouldn't that have been an exciting career?). There's no doubt in my mind that a combination of doctor-prescribed medication and naturopath-recommended regular vibe plate use (I ended up purchasing my own) accounted for my initial healing following my BMT.

I also received some questionable advice from well-meaning caregivers. A little while after the Gang had its way with my tendons by tightening and shortening them up good, I was referred to a physiatrist. Physiatrists are medical doctors, physical medicine and rehabilitation (PM&R) physicians to be exact. They treat a wide variety of medical conditions affecting the brain, spinal cord, nerves, bones, joints, ligaments, muscles and tendons. My parents accompanied me on my first visit, and the doctor told us about a treatment that could help relieve the tightness in my tendons, giving me more range of motion throughout my body.

The treatment was called photochemotherapy (PUVA), and it mostly treats skin-related diseases like psoriasis and eczema. Medication is given forty-five minutes to an hour before skin is exposed to ultraviolet light. Patients must wear their birthday suits for maximum exposure and goggles to protect their eyes from radiation while standing in a cabinet containing twenty-four or more six-foot-long UVA fluorescent lights. Cabinet stays increase over time, starting at about one minute and increasing for up to half an hour. Treatments must be at least forty-eight hours apart to avoid excessive skin redness or burning. After about fifteen treatments, there should be a significant improvement, but the therapy isn't always effective. If there's no improvement after thirty treatments, they're usually stopped.

Wow, the potential for significant improvement after only fifteen treatments—that's like six weeks if I got treatments every forty-eight hours! Sure, PUVA isn't always effective, but is there ever a 100 per cent guarantee that a treatment will work? Score one big point for going for it. However, PUVA had a potential to cause skin cancer, including melanomas. Photoaging, which makes the skin dry and wrinkled due to pigment alterations called lentigines, was a strong likelihood. Other potential side effects included burning, itching skin, and eye damage. Well alrighty then, that's a whole lotta points against taking the plunge. After we left the physiatrist's office, my parents and I talked it over for about five seconds. I called the doctor, thanked him for his time and said I would pass.

Role Reversal

There have been a few opportunities during my hospital stays and outpatient visits when I could help medical caregivers build their skills. As I mentioned earlier, there's nothin' like the real thing, baby, and this is certainly true regarding textbook images and videos versus hands-on procedures and seeing the effects of an infection or disease in person. When that intern attempted to extract a sample of stem cells from my hipbone and wasn't successful, it was still a valuable learning opportunity for him. Dr. S once asked me if it was OK for a group of interns to stop by and see the toll the Gang was taking on my tendons, muscles and joints. It was a little uncomfortable when they started moving my extremities around like I was one of those jointed wooden figures you sometimes see in pain relief commercials.

But this was nothing compared with the time I developed an abscess between my butt cheeks. It was super uncomfortable and made sitting difficult; however, even more uncomfortable was when Dr. S asked if some interns could stop by and have a look.

Say what? Young interns probing the inside of my butt crack?

Surely there was a someone—anyone—with a similar infection somewhere in the hospital who could be the guinea pig. Dr. S could tell that I was hesitant, and he assured me that both he and the interns would completely understand if I refused. I can be stoic at times when I'm like jelly inside, so I finally agreed. I laid flat on my stomach on the examination table with my hospital gown open at the back. I kept my eyes shut and clenched my fists while Dr. S spread my buns for all to see.

Family Ties

These are just some of the accounts of the stellar care I've received from and sometimes provided to medical caregivers. Of course, there are a number of non-medical heroes who have supported me as well. Aside from my parents and grandmas, there were three other people who made me feel "normal" in situations that were anything but: Ted, Mike, and my friend Julie.

Ted and I have similar personalities—we're both strong-willed and like to have our way. We fought a lot, both verbally and physically, when growing up. Remember, Ted is five years older than me and he was always in good shape. I was a strong kid, but I was never a match for him in a physical fight. Nonetheless, I still tried; pulling hair was my best move. We also liked to one up each other, mainly on the topic of who was smarter. My dad and Mike are practically geniuses and my mom is also extremely smart, thus, the battle was over who was the dumbest in the family. Once when my dad caught us shouting at each other at the top of our lungs, he dished out the worst possible punishment by making us hug it out—mutual *ewww*!

We didn't always fight. In fact, we had a lot more in common than our strong-willed personalities. We both liked being active and playing sports. Ted was the ultimate sportsman, and both Mike and I looked up to him. I listened to whatever music he liked, including his favourite hard rock early eighties bands when most kids my age were listening to Sharon, Lois & Bram. He taught me how to build snow forts and throw snowballs that would hit their mark. He even taught me how to ride a bike. And then proceeded to ditch me, taking off with his friend the first time I didn't wipe out after ten seconds. I ended up having to take Grade 13 calculus by correspondence, and Ted helped me get an A.

Teasing their little sister was a favourite pastime for my brothers, although I'd like to say that I gave as good as I got. They were always trying to get a rise out of me by calling me babyish names in a demeaning voice. Actually, my dad started it all because he rarely called me by my given name; it was always silly names like "Boogie" or "Doodle." My brothers picked up on this, and they'd either mimic the names my dad used or make up their own names like "Poopster" and "Precious" (the name that bothered me the most).

At the beginning of this book, I talked about Ted calling me "Leukemia Chick" on a day when I was feeling particularly freakish. This should have made me feel even more freakish, but instead, it had the opposite effect and I started laughing. Humour was often key to lightening up my dark moods, and it usually made me feel much better. I don't recall Ted ever calling me that name again, but it has always stuck in my mind. Hence the book title and, like that day, I laugh when I think about it.

Normalcy was hugely important to me throughout my first two journeys with The Big C. Whether or not he had to make a conscious effort, Ted's demeanour towards me rarely changed, even when I was in full BABUDEEP mode. He still teased me and talked with me about everyday things. We also still fought and tried to one up each other, as usual. My parents told me that Ted really wanted to be my donor (he was close, a 4/6 match), and although he was thrilled that a perfect match was found, he was disappointed that it was Mike instead of him. The normalcy Ted brought to my abnormal life was just as important to my health as the treatments. My best friend Shawn and my closest cousin were the same, providing the normalcy I so craved when I was with them.

I've often used the words "well meaning" and "unintentionally" in this book. These words also apply to those whose non-verbal communication and body language communicated both pity over my situation and alarm when they encountered me at various BABUDEEP stages. Mike, who wears his huge heart on his sleeve, would often do double takes and stare at me, eyes filled with fear and concern, when he thought I wasn't looking. We have always been close. Although we were almost two years apart in age, we were usually the same height as kids, and some people would ask if we were twins. We had a lot of the same friends in high school and participated in many of the same after-school activities like concert band, jazz band and school plays. Ted started his first year of university when I started Grade 9, and it was comforting to still have an older brother around to support me as I entered high school as a bundle of nerves, a basket case and a nervous wreck all rolled into one.

Mike is much less strong-willed than Ted and me; he's a lot like my mom, who is more willing to go with the flow. Not to say that Mike and I didn't have our fights, they were just less physical. Mike was a master at coming up with the most ridiculous and annoying names to drive me crazy. Somehow, he came up with the name "Poonie," and once some of our mutual friends picked up on it, there was no escape.

As adults, Mike and I have spent a lot of time together and we keep in regular touch. It probably helps that we're both single, never married and have no children. After my parents, Mike's the one with whom I share any health-related information. We also have similar music interests, and we've attended many concerts together, including three concerts that were twenty years apart. At each one we were movin' and groovin' to the tunes of my favourite band of all time, Tears for Fears. While Ted is a sports nut, Mike's a travel nut, and thanks to him, I've enjoyed several memorable trips with him both nationally and internationally that I'll expand on in later in the book.

When it comes to food, Mike is an aficionado who loves to cook and bake and is talented at it. This works out well for us because I'd rather clean up. Despite my stubbornness, Mike has often forced me outside of my tiny food comfort zone. He's fond of some of the craziest sounding and looking Asian cuisine—chicken feet, anyone? I hate to admit it, but he is usually right when he says that I'll like something, and after I finally give in and try it, it becomes a favourite.

What is a Friend, Anyway?

One of my closest friends (I'll call her Julie) was an absolute rock throughout my breast cancer diagnosis. We met about eighteen years ago when we worked for the same company that runs several private retirement and long-term care (LTC) homes throughout Ontario. The facility we worked at housed a retirement home (Julie's hood) and an LTC home (my hood). Julie is one of the few people whom I fully trust and feel completely comfortable with in any situation. I had some issues with a new administrator that caused me a lot of anxiety and doubt in my abilities. Julie and a few other staff members were well aware of what was going on, and she led the charge in shielding and supporting me throughout the entire ordeal.

Julie was also at my side when Dr. D revealed my initial breast cancer diagnosis. My parents had scheduled a vacation long before, and I encouraged them to go as I had not yet had all of the tests and it would take a while to get the results. However, Dr. D's nurse called me about an appointment to get my test results sooner than expected. Although they wouldn't have made it home in time to attend, I knew that if I told them, they would cut their vacation short. I also knew that Julie would be the ideal substitute, and when I called her, she was more than happy to accompany me.

Similar to the doomsday appointments when Dr. S confirmed my ALL diagnosis and relapse, my mind started reeling when Dr. D confirmed that I had breast cancer. With my mind back in the unpleasant side of la-la land, Dr. D's explanation of the next steps mostly went in one ear and out the other. After the appointment, Julie kindly offered to take me to a local coffee shop to unwind and process the situation. It wasn't long before we were both laughing. Julie had remembered pretty much all of the post-diagnosis steps Dr. D talked about and offered to write them down for me. After a long search through her purse, she found a pen but nothing to write on. I didn't have anything either, so the first steps of my breast cancer journey ended up being beautifully written on a bunch of restaurant napkins.

Two of my special caregivers (and mentors) don't even know me or that they've been helping me navigate life's difficulties for decades. In my research, I came across a blog post entitled "Can You Truly Be Friends with Someone You Have Never Met in Person?" Numerous people answered the question, and many made the following point which spoke to me: "Although we may only make a strong connection with someone when we can look them in the eye, we should consider a friend to be anyone we feel a connection with who brings something positive into our lives." I totally agree! This is particularly true when we make friends through social media where there's little chance of ever meeting in person.

My mom introduced me to a young American woman named Joni Eareckson Tada through her books and music when I was about ten. When she was seventeen, Joni broke her neck after diving off a floating dock into shallow water. She became a quadriplegic. Even though she was much closer to my mom's age, I was drawn to this courageous woman who turned to God for the strength to rise above her tragic accident and trust that He had a wonderful plan for her life. Little did she know that this plan included a ministry called Joni and Friends that provides mobility, dignity and the hope of God's Word worldwide through its many programs. One program, Wheels for the World, collects wheelchairs and other mobility devices that are restored to like-new condition and distributed to individuals living in poverty around the world. Over ten thousand devices are custom fit to recipients each year. It's not lost on me that I bonded with Joni over ten years before I developed a disability that I continue to need God's strength to rise above.

During my first two journeys with The Big C, there were many nights when I laid on my hospital bed in physical and/or emotional pain, unable to sleep. On these nights, I often got out my Walkman and listened to Joni's music. Her beautiful, calming voice singing songs of God's hope and love lulled me to sleep. Today, Joni provides four-minute podcasts on weekdays that I can access on the *Joni and Friends* website. Like anyone else, I still have days when I get the blues, but I rarely have physical pain anymore. No matter how I'm feeling, I listen to all of Joni's inspiring messages, often after I get into bed. Joni's positive and calming voice continues to speak God-inspired words of love and hope that are such a comfort.

Now in her early seventies, Joni has suffered for years with chronic, often excruciating, pain from over fifty years in a wheelchair. She is also dealing with stage three breast cancer treatment that causes even more pain. It's uber-humbling when Joni talks about how she is humbled by people who are bedridden and suffer from chronic pain at a much higher frequency and level compared to hers.

Joni is an extremely positive and upbeat person, but she's quick to point out that leading a Christian life and following God's Word doesn't equate with a shiny, happy life or require a shiny, happy persona 24/7. She also emphasizes that God expects us to complain, get angry, feel sorry for ourselves and question why He allows suffering. Like a good parent, God doesn't demand perfection from His children; rather, He comforts us and builds us up.

In my early forties, I was introduced to an older American woman named Joyce Meyer through church friends. Like Joni's story, recalling Joyce's account of the heartbreaking life challenges she's faced brings me to my figurative knees in utter humility when I focus on the "have-nots." From the time she was a little girl and into her mid-teens, Joyce was regularly sexually abused, mostly by her alcoholic father but also by other family members as well. Her mother knew about the abuse, but it wasn't until a few years before her death when she finally admitted that she did nothing for fear of the scandal it would cause. When Joyce was eighteen, she married the first man who showed any interest in her, and for the next five years, her nightmarish life continued. Her husband physically and mentally abused her, stole from her and didn't even try to hide his regular infidelity. He even left her stranded with no money to pay for a ride home when they'd travel to different locations around the country.

Although she invited Jesus into her heart at age nine, Joyce convinced herself that the abuse and mistreatment happened because there was something wrong with her. She never expected or felt she deserved any blessings in her life. Her negative attitude and lack of self-worth made her a bitter and angry woman. It wasn't until about twenty years into her second marriage that Joyce's journey towards self-acceptance began. She learned that God's love is unconditional and that accepting it is not only something that we can do to find joy in everyday life (the name of her weekday television show), it's something God's Word asks us to do.

Around this time, Joyce began a series of small, local Bible studies that have since grown into a worldwide ministry. Like Joni, she's quick to add that both she and her life are far from perfect and that she still struggles with things like impatience, unforgiveness and selfishness. Joyce's transparency is part of what drew me to her. I started reading her books and listening to her speak on her weekday television show a few years before being diagnosed with breast cancer. She always includes herself among those who often stray from the path God has designed for our lives, but she encourages everyone to follow Jesus' example by finding ways to help and forgive others rather than judge and hold grudges. She also speaks of how God's love is not only unconditional but equal and available for all.

Joyce's worldwide ministry includes programs like Hands of Hope that serves people living in impoverished countries. Project GRL is a Hands of Hope outreach for girls and young women worldwide who have been mistreated, marginalized or feel insecure or hopeless. Within Project GRL, an anti human trafficking program rescues women and girls from peril in fourteen countries around the world. Another outreach drills freshwater wells to replace the disease-infested waters women and girls in developing countries often spend their entire day gathering to bring back to their families. Having much closer access to clean water opens up time for educational opportunities that Joyce's ministry also provides.

A Different Perspective

Joni and Joyce are among the many caregivers I've turned to and found a fresh and humbling perspective, especially when my pity parties wake up the neighbours. The last thing I want is for people to feel sorry for me. Feeling pity is natural, and it's not done with negative intent, but I want readers to understand why they shouldn't pity me. The first synonym for the word "sympathy" that showed up on my computer thesaurus was "pity." When I plugged in the word "empathy," the first words that showed up were "understanding" and "compassion." I continue to practice replacing pity with empathy and compassion.

My life has been full of blessings that would take an anthology to cover, and in the next chapter, I've isolated some of my experiences that have made for a full and fulfilling life.

CHAPTER NINE:
IT WAS THE BEST OF TIMES ...

My Cottage is My Castle: On Chesley Lake

I wanted to start with the Murray cottage, as it trumps all blessings. Both sides of my extended family were fairly close in the emotional sense. While my mom's side were fairly close in distance as well—Owen Sound, Newmarket and Toronto—my dad's side, not so much—Aylmer (near London) and Sarnia. This may be why Grandma Murray (from Aylmer) decided to purchase a family cottage where we could get together during the summer and on holidays like Thanksgiving.

My dad assisted her in finding a suitable cottage, and we went as a family to check out the option. Although it was located about a half-hour drive from Owen Sound and my grandma lived so far away, she decided on a cottage located on Chesley Lake, about a ten-minute drive to Sauble Beach on Lake Huron. What the cottage may have lacked in structure and plumbing, it more than made up for in property features. While we had close neighbours on one side, everything was completely covered by trees and bushes and there were no neighbours on the other side, only an open field—so we're talking pri-va-cy, man!

There was a good sized lawn, but the pièce de résistance was the long wooden dock with private access to the gorgeous lake. The dock was T-shaped, and there was a metal ladder leading into the water on one side. You could also get into the water via a flat stone area located at the bottom on the stairs. Thankfully, the water had a stony bottom instead of those mushy ones that feel so gross and are full of leeches.

When I see the inside of gorgeous cottages in the Muskokas and Kawarthas, they just don't seem like cottages to me. Aside from a sturdier structure and better plumbing, there's nothing I'd change about the Murray cottage—and we're talking mismatched, mostly uncomfortable furniture, a tiny kitchen and eating area, and no TV. There were two tiny bedrooms, one with a bunk bed and the other with two twin beds. My brothers got the bunk beds while I was beside them in one of the twin beds. The larger bedroom had a full-sized bed, and the couch in the living room area was a pull-out. If you wanted a private conversation you'd either have to whisper or go outside because the walls were paper-thin—something we enjoyed as kids as we'd talk to each other through the walls until my dad yelled at us to stop it (you didn't want him to tell you twice).

We didn't even have a shower installed for several years, but we were just kids and couldn't care less. Isn't that what the lake is for?

Candyland

When you first turned onto the road leading to our cottage area, there was a sign that said Chesley Lake Mennonite Camp. There was a left turn onto a gravel road that led to our cottage, but if you kept going straight down the road, you'd come to the camp area. The camp had a trailer park, cottages to rent, a private beach area, a golf course, a marina, a church, a playground, a baseball diamond ... but it also had a main building that had the equivalent to the O&J in candy. The tuck shop also sold comic books and cheesy, dusty knick-knacks that never seemed to sell. Just outside the tuck shop you could choose from several flavours of mouth-watering ice cream that you could enjoy on a cone (three scoops, please) or as a triple decker sundae in the adjoining restaurant.

Miss Scarlet on the Playground with the Popsicle

Mike and I enjoyed devouring our tuck shop treasures at the playground. The wooden play structure with all the different levels and room-like areas to climb around in became the "stage" for games of Clue—you know, the murder-mystery board game with Professor Plum and his pals?—whenever our two cousins from Sarnia were staying with us. The problem was that my female cousins and I all wanted to be Miss Scarlet because she was the prettiest. I don't recall us ever even starting our live re-enactment of the game. Referring to the play structure as a "stage" was appropriate as Mike would, hilariously, sometimes cast himself as Mrs. Peacock and get us laughing our butts off. This calmed the Miss Scarlet skirmishes.

A Surprise Gift

Mike and I practically lived in the lake, taking breaks only for lunch and maybe a short respite for a snack and to read comics. One year when we reached the end of the long, steep gravel staircase from the parked car for our first summer stay at the cottage, we found a huge inner tube sitting there. We might as well have struck gold because it became our most valued piece of water play equipment. We couldn't wait to get our bathing suits on, throw the tube into the lake and then jump on it. We could sit on either side and bounce up and down until someone fell off, and we'd wrap our arms around it as we kicked our legs underwater to venture farther and farther away from the dock.

King of the dock was another favourite for us, especially because my dad and Ted sometimes joined us. What could be better than Mike and I (pretty much the same size and weight) climbing up the dock ladder and getting thrown off the end time after time by my dad or Ted. It was much more of a challenge when it was me against Mike or my dad against Ted (when Ted got a little older, that is). Inevitably, there were the odd scrapes and bruises—Mom always thought Dad and Ted were being too rough—but we always got over it.

On the Game

We also spent a lot of time playing board games, especially on rainy days. There were the classics: Monopoly, Life, Clue, Battleship, Yahtzee, Mastermind. Hey Gen X, remember Full House, Payday, and the pop-up timed games Perfection and Super Perfection?

There was another game called Pit that we played as a family around the dinner table. It could get pretty wild. All the players were commodity traders trying to corner the market on a commodity (e.g., wheat, barley, corn) by making a series of blind trades. When the market is cornered on a commodity, trading stops and points are tallied. Players play simultaneously, encouraging a frenzied atmosphere, and you need to get loud and even a little pushy if you've any hope of winning, Those poor cards took a beating as everyone slammed them onto the table yelling, "1, 1, 1!" or, "3, 3, 3!" even, "5, 5, 5!" desperate to find those last few cards that would fill your hand of eight with a single commodity so you could ring the bell and shout, "Pit!" to confirm victory.

Card games were also popular, and one in particular was perfect for multiple participants. When the grammas, grampas, cousins and friends were up, our after-dinner entertainment was often a rousing card game called 21-31. Each player receives three pennies and is dealt three cards. Players can only have three cards in their hand at any time. On their turn, players can pick up the card that's facing up, add it to their hand and discard something else face-up, or draw a card and either add it to their hand or discard it face up. The goal was to achieve a score of 31, meaning you have an ace (worth 11 points) and two of a combination of queens, jacks or 10s (worth 10 points each) for each suit. However, when you have a score of 21 or more you can "knock," which indicates that the next round is the last one. Whoever has the lowest score must pay a penny, and if there's a tie, the suit worth the most wins. Spades is highest, followed by hearts, diamonds and clubs. After you pay your third penny, you're "on your honour" and you're out after the next loss. I encourage you to try it at your next family event or party.

Then there was the "game" we played at the dinner table while we were eating. This was a punishment game for breaking dinnertime etiquette by putting your elbows on the table. It was perfect for tattletales. With eagle eyes, we would monitor each other's every move, hoping to catch someone with at least one elbow on the table. When someone was caught, Mike for example, the rest of us would chant, "Mike, Mike, strong and able, get your elbows off the table. This is not a horse's stable, but a fancy dining table—stand up, stand up!" We'd decide on a punishment for the heinous crime, which usually meant the culprit had to walk around the cottage outside several times. On one rare occasion, we caught my mom and dad at the same time and their punishment was to walk around the cottage with my mom on my dad's back—classic!

Drive, Drive, Drive Your Boat, Quickly Down the Lake

We had a cottage, we had a dock, we had a lake, and soon enough, we had a boat. It was a used speedboat, white with a powder blue front that had a white stripe down the middle. The motor was a 55 horsepower Evinrude (named after the firefly in one of my favourite childhood animated movies, *The Rescuers*—or vice versa?). My parents already had waterskis, and we got child-sized ones for Christmas one year. I was as excited as on Christmas morning when my parents would announce that it was a waterskiing day.

Everyone in the family could get up on the skis, usually on the first try. My parents, and later Ted, could go with one ski. I tried but never mastered it before the boat was sold. However, crossing the wake was the best feeling. I can still envision looking at my dad or Ted driving the boat and my mom or Mike watching to see if I fell. I always had a huge smile on my face. That smile would turn into a wince when I got an unwanted enema as a stream of water slid sharply through my butt crack—*owie powie!* Ted could also put the handle behind his knees and, of course, little sister had to try it too. Need I say more?

Beach Bums

Where to start on Sauble Beach? How about the huge red-and-white-striped slide we could pay to slide down on a burlap sack. By the late seventies'- and small-town kids'- standards it was quite the attraction. There was also a place close to the beach that had multiple small square trampolines built into the floor. The best was when there were only a few people there and we could hop from one tramp to the other because they were so close together. That is, until staff spotted us and gave us heck for straying from our assigned tramp.

Across from the jumping joint was the arcade—two giant, smoky, sandy-floored rooms that would make any pinball wizard drool with delight, although it wasn't long until games like Evel Knievel, The Six-Million Dollar Man and Charlie's Angels were evicted. This was the dawn of arcade video games: Space Invaders, Galaxian, Asteroids, and, later, Pac-Man, Frogger, and Donkey Kong. You name it, they had it. This was definitely Ted's forte, and, unlike his little sister, he could make a quarter last far past the first few levels. Mike wasn't so bad either.

In the early '80s, a water slide was added, which gave the arcade a run for its money. Even Canada's Wonderland didn't have a water park at that time! Up the high, steep staircase, down the slide countless times—sitting up, backwards, lying on our backs and tummies. The two lifeguards at the top never allowed us to stand up like we wanted to, though, as attempts were met with threats of ejection from the park.

The go-karts were another attraction where you risked getting banned if you got too aggressive. Come on, racing against my brothers? Perfect opportunity for little sis to cut 'em off and zoom past to victory. It was a blast and I fulfilled my need for speed until that fateful day when my need was off the charts and instead of veering off to the left to stay on the track, I veered off to the right and slammed into a bunch of waiting karts. I wasn't hurt physically, but I was utterly humiliated and never darkened the doors of the raceway again.

Last but not least, the beach. Lake Huron is one of the colder Great Lakes, but we had built up an immunity and spent hours riding the waves that got high on windy days. When we weren't in the water, we were building sandcastles or burying someone in the sand (trying to anyway). After hours, when it was getting dark and definitely too cold to swim, our parents would splurge for fries on the beach. They were a Sauble Beach must-have while watching the sun set over the lake, which was breathtaking (even for a kid).

Celebrity Sighting in the Hampton

Two other popular destinations near Chesley Lake were Port Elgin and Southampton. Port Elgin had a great drive-in theatre where we could see the latest flicks. We'd often get in our PJs and make popcorn to take. We'd also take our pillows and blankets to get comfortable while we stretched out in the back seats and my parents reclined the front seats so they could get comfortable and we could see. I don't know if we ever stayed for the entire second show.

The movie *Fame* was the second show once. My dad and I both liked the TV version and used to watch it together. However, a woman in the movie who didn't get accepted to The High School for Performing Arts shouted obscenities that would make a sailor blush, so my dad hightailed it outta there.

Southampton had great cigar shops with racks of comic books and scads of sweets. It's also famous for beautiful beaches that my mom spent a lot of time at in the summers of her childhood and teenage years. My grams and gramps were good friends with Charles and Olive Short, who also spent many summers in the Hampton. My mom was good friends with their oldest daughter, Nora, and her youngest sister hung around with Nora's youngest brother, Marty. Yep, that's Martin Short, the comedian from Hamilton, Ontario, who grew in fame when he joined the cast of *Second City TV* (*SCTV*) and subsequently *Saturday Night Live*. My mom and Nora sometimes babysat her youngest sister and Marty, and she said his crazy antics were there from the start.

Cottage for the Holidays

Up until I was about to enter Grade 10, my family spent every labour day weekend at the cottage. One of the three families that formed the Murray Church (more on this in Chapter Fifteen) and another family with a son who was Mike's age and a daughter who was a year younger than Ted (I'll call them Grant and Justine) joined us. That left six adults and seven to nine kids (more when girlfriends and other friends showed up).

Fright Night

Although Justine was four years older than me, she was the only other girl, so the two of us mostly hung around with Mike and Grant. Ted and the older kids went their own way and usually ignored us, but at times they would lower themselves and walk with the unworthy younger kids to and from the main camp area.

One night there was a special event at the camp church and when it was over we all walked home together. One of the older boys was into horror movies and he gave a detailed overview of one of his favourite frightening flicks. Justine and I were totally freaked out, holding on tightly to each other. To add to the freak factor, aside from a few dim cottage lights here and there, it was pitch-dark as we walked down the desolate dirt roads. Suddenly, what might well have been one of the hounds of hell jumped out of the darkness, barking loudly, stopping us in our tracks. The guys would never admit it, but they screamed just as loudly and shrilly as us girls, scaring the beast away.

Food, Glorious Food

One of the best parts of the weekend was all the mouth-watering sweet and savoury food. There were three mothers who were uber-talented cooks and bakers, plus some brilliant BBQers among the dads, which made for a smorgasbord that would turn any TV chef's insults into accolades. Most of the delectable desserts were pre-made, and there was one particular delicacy called Black & White Dessert. It was a chocolate cookie crumble base with vanilla custard filling and half chocolate, half vanilla tempered frosting on top. Pure bliss!

With all that food came the need for a lot of meal preparation and clean-up assistance. With so many people around, meals were always buffet style and everyone but the cooks had to draw from a myriad of tasks. The tasks were supposed to require equal time and effort, but come on, everyone knows that getting out the dinnerware and placing it at the top of the buffet table was the easiest—five minutes tops.

Sex Education

The large number of people present also made for creative bedtime arrangements. One of the families brought a tent trailer that slept five, the other adults were on the double bed in one of the bedrooms and the pull-out couch in the living room. Ted got his own room, and Justine, Grant, Mike and I switched between the other bedroom and sleeping bags on the hard living room floor. That is, when the older siblings of the older boys, their girlfriends and other friends weren't present. Then, the younger kids were kicked out of the cottage and into a small tent on the lumpy lawn.

I vividly recall one night when the four of us were in the tent and the adults were out on the deck chatting. The adults could hear everything we said, which didn't enter my thoughts as my innocent and curious mind saw the perfect opportunity to ask the three older kids about the meaning of a term I'd recently heard an older girl from the 2nd Avenue Gang using. The term starts with "sc" and rhymes with "brewing"—can you image what came next? Well, I can only imagine what Mike's and Justine's faces looked like as I blurted out the question, but Grant calmly and confidently gave me a definition that was mostly off the mark. Guess who got the dreaded "birds and the bees" talk after we got home?

Super Dad

Thanksgiving weekend was the other holiday my family always spent at the cottage. Mostly my mom's side of the family joined us: gramma, grampa, aunt and cousin. Timing was good because there were more people around to help my dad close up the cottage for the winter. My mom, gramma and aunt would huddle-up on the stone surface above the water and cheer on their hero as he waded knee-deep into freezing cold water to disconnect the water hose.

Footballs & Feasts

The fall leaves were especially vibrant at Chesley Lake, and while the turkey was cooking, we'd venture out on a long trail walk. Ted always brought a football, and he, my dad and my cousin would toss it back and forth. Much to their dismay, my dad would insist that Mike and I—the kids who didn't have a quarterback's arm—join in when we got the notion.

There was always way more food than the lot of us could eat, although Mike and my aunt would try and break the trend when they made a wager on who could eat the most. I love me some turkey and fixins', but I most looked forward to the home-made pumpkin pie. My mom is the pumpkin pie queen, and she always added a big dollop of whipped cream—which was my job to make—on top, so it melted in my mouth.

Benedict Bunker

We were pretty competitive in our games of 21-31 (who wouldn't be for a pot of three pennies per person?), and once someone was out, they'd choose someone who was still in to cheer on. One rare Thanksgiving weekend when my dad's middle brother and family were up (the "Clue cousins"), it was down to me and one of the cousins. My grampa—yes, my flesh and blood on my mother's side of the family—was cheering for my cousin on the Murray side instead of his only granddaughter. I was not amused. Wait just a second, Buster, she has her own grampa—you traitor!

End of Eden

We were devastated when my gramma sold the Murray cottage, although she was more than justified. Everyone was getting older, the "kids" were getting jobs and doing their own thing over the summer. My dad pretty much did all of the grunt work, and I don't think my gramma felt as safe and confident as she once did driving to the cottage and spending time there on her own.

CHAPTER TEN:
IT WAS THE WORST OF TIMES

Pomp & Circumstances

You may be wondering why I'm writing about "the worst of times" instead of focusing exclusively on "the best of times." I promise that I'll get back to the good stuff, but there are some worst-of-times experiences related to The Big C that I thought would be of interest to you. Perhaps it will also underscore why I've grown to believe that life experiences don't all have to be positive to make for a fulfilling life.

You know that bouts with Dr. P and HWMNBN and the visible signs they left on my face coincided with Grade 13 grad. Remember the eye patch? Ahoy ye maties! Well, my Grade 8 graduation also occurred at an inopportune time, and I wasn't sure whether or not I'd be able to attend one or both of the events.

I wrote earlier that I was sprung from the joint about two weeks before the end of my Grade 8 school year. My energy level wasn't where I wanted it to be and—shocker—neither was my appearance. I wasn't in full Dr. P mode, but I was wearing bandanas and hats to cover up my balding head. Despite my indecision, my parents offered to buy me a new graduation outfit. This was the "more is more" eighties, and pastels and bold patterns were in. I remember going to a local store and choosing an embroidered, pastel pink skirt and blazer set. A plain white blouse I already had would suffice to wear underneath the blazer, but it was in dire need of some bling. My eyes were drawn to the glowing and gaudy jewelry section, and I picked out a trendy brooch with three large, flashy, pastel-coloured stones to pin at my neck. My outfit wouldn't have been complete without a pair of nylons, but not just any nylons—the kind that were embroidered with bold patterns.

Grad day arrived and I was still agonizing over whether or not I should go. My dad was pushing me to go, but he was a guy and didn't understand how important appearance was for a vain teenager. The huge issue of my sparse hair was somewhat resolved a few days before when I found one of my mom's dress hats (which were in at the time), tried it on and decided that it would do a decent job of hiding the baldest areas of my head. I honestly wasn't feeling great, but I have to admit that I likely had enough energy to at least attend the ceremony. In the end, I decided not to go and it was one of those unfortunate times when I gave into my foolish, appearance-related pride and missed a good opportunity.

The next day I found I had won the history award, one of only two awards that I was qualified to win. While I didn't inherit my mom's excellent sewing and cooking genes, my dad is a historian, and I got a good helping of those genes. A close friend accepted the award on my behalf, and she stopped by my house early the next day to tell me about my win and bring me the trophy. I was happy to hear that I'd won the award, but my spirits dampened as she told me about how much fun I missed and how so many people wanted to see me.

I did get to experience the whole grad thing—dress, date, corsage, dinner, dancing, after-party, the whole shebang—when I was in Grade 12. My best friend Shawn was graduating from Grade 13, and I was hanging out mostly with his friends, who became my friends. Grade 12 students were welcome to attend, and I wanted to be there with my friends. I had a great time, and most of my friends also had "friend dates," so we all hung around together. There were several after-parties, and we changed out of our fancy grad duds before heading to a party at a rural location that had a huge bonfire in one of the fields. We mingled with other friends for a while and then laid down blankets near the bonfire and talked until we fell asleep.

When we all woke up around dawn, my date was concerned that my dad (who intimidated many of my friends, usually unintentionally) would be angry with him for keeping his daughter out all night. I was also a little concerned because I wasn't absolutely certain that lifting my curfew meant that my date could return me home the next day. However, I assured my date that he had nothing to worry about. I was right because there were no cop cars waiting to arrest him for kidnapping when he dropped me off at my house.

When It Rains, It Pours

If you knew a bunch of bad things were headed your way, would you rather have everything happen over one year or spread out over several years? Not sure? Me neither, especially if someone asked me that question in 1990, the best year of my teenage life and the year before the worst year of my teenage life. The year 1991 was one that disproved the idiom, "Lightning never strikes twice." The Big C relapse in March (back to Sick Kids for more chemo and radiation), intense chemo and radiation before a BMT in April, acute GvHD symptoms that signalled a jump to chronic GvHD, the death of my grandma on my mom's side on June 28, HWMNBN in October and, finally, my grandma on my dad's side passing on December 30. No more grandparents (my grandpas passed in 1975 and 1981). Poor me, huh? Yes, it was a tough year.

Varsity Blues

Although my science skills were moderate, I was in enrolled in the honours bachelor of science health studies co-op program at the University of Waterloo (UW). The school was famous for offering a co-op option where you could alternate a semester of study and a semester of working in your field while completing your degree. Thus, it would take me five rather than four years to graduate. I can't blame Ted, whom I looked up to, for my choosing a program with required courses that I knew would be challenging for me. Ted's a math and science guy to the core, and he often told me about the merits of studying in this area, but I made my choice (that I would later rethink) of my own free will.

At first, I couldn't wait to start my fall 1992 semester. I figured that the BABUDEEP would have stopped haunting me by then (or would at least spend more time in hiding) and I'd be back on my way to my "normal" self. Although my hair had a ways to go before it was long again, my bangs would be long enough to sufficiently cover my HWMNBN scars.

But by late May, my positive thoughts took a turn towards the negative as things weren't improving at the speed I'd hoped. Three months later, aside from my bangs, improvements were still not enough in my uber-critical eyes. Fear started to grow inside me at an alarming pace, and after my parents dropped me off at residence the day before Frosh Week began, my fears were in maximum overdrive.

The typical Frosh Week experience, according to friends who had gone before, is the most radical and exciting week of a first year college or university student's life. It involves parties with new friends, having drinks together, engaging in cheesy dance routines, attending concerts and playing games. I missed it all because I did my best to avoid almost all of it. One exception involved a group for students on campus called InterVarsity Christian Fellowship. I attended and enjoyed a few of their events, and I even met some friends, but the friendships waned a few months into the first semester.

Making friends was forefront on my mind, but my mind was also occupied with concerns about navigating the huge campus when classes started the following week. The science and arts buildings at UW were almost at opposite ends of campus, and many of the buildings were quite spread out. All of my electives were in the arts area, and it would be quite a hike when I had to attend back-to-back classes at opposite ends of campus. But it wasn't until towards the end of my first year that I began to notice that walking long distances was becoming a bit of a struggle.

I first noticed it when a friend was going to drive me home for the weekend and I had to walk from my residence all the way to the opposite side of campus to meet her. When I arrived, I was gasping for air. Naturally, this startled me and my friend, but after I got my breath back, I didn't think much of it. After all, I was carrying a heavy bag on my shoulder whereas I normally carried only a backpack with a few textbooks inside. Towards the end of the second semester, I noticed that even carrying my backpack across campus winded me much sooner than usual. Worse, at times, my legs would start to feel like jelly to the extent where I thought they were going to give out before I reached my destination.

First year ended and I barely passed several of my science and math courses. However, I did exceptionally well in my arts electives, and this gave my average a boost. I also needed a boost, as even more strange things were happening with my body. I was finding it harder to climb stairs, especially the high and steep ones. Bending over to tie my shoes or pick up something I dropped was also becoming a challenge.

These challenges became more evident while I was working at a golf course outside of Shelburne over the summer. Stairs were everywhere—into the clubhouse, up to the manager's office and down to the storeroom. A lot of bending and reaching was required, and all of this was becoming a problem for me.

A Forced Gap Year

I was anxious to get out of student housing in my second year at UW. Mike, who also attended UW and was home from his UW sister-university stay in Germany, was looking for a place to live for his fifth and final year. We decided to look for a place together and soon found a three-bedroom basement apartment that we would share with another student. The walk to campus was a lot farther than my walk from my first-year residence, but reaching campus was only half the walk, as most of my morning classes were held in buildings on the opposite side. Thus, I had to get up earlier, and I'm not a morning person. The point is that I was getting winded and jelly-legged much more frequently than towards the end of my first year.

Most of my first-and second-year courses were in huge auditoriums to accommodate hundreds of students. Desks were arranged along several levels leading to the bottom level where professors had their desks and gave their lectures. In my first year, I would randomly choose where to sit, as the level didn't matter. However, in my second year, my seating options became limited to the top two levels. When I entered the auditorium on my first day of classes, I sat down at a desk located on a mid-level. The professor asked us to come down, one level at a time, to retrieve several handouts that were piled on his desk, and I found it difficult to climb back up the steps to my seat. It was equally difficult to climb the steps back up to the main level at the end of class. As you know, I hate asking for help, but from that day on, I asked students who were sitting near me if they wouldn't mind retrieving handouts or taking my assignments and completed tests with them when necessary.

I didn't have to endure these challenges for long. Around the time the Toronto Blue Jays won their second consecutive World Series on October 23, 1993—go Jays go!—I came home after a long day of classes and went directly to my bedroom to lie down. Earlier in the day, I started experiencing some discomfort in the left side of my chest that had turned into mild pain. The pain was worse the next day, but I didn't want to tell Mike, the worrier. Instead, I called my parents and described what was going on. I knew they wouldn't want me to wait to see if things got better when the pain was in the same area as my heart, so it wasn't the least bit surprising when they came to pick me up that same day. However, I never imagined that would be the end of my second year at UW.

The pain (and worry) was intensifying after my parents drove me to the local hospital. It turned out that I must have caught some sort of virus because there was fluid building up around my heart. I'm glad the doctors held off telling me that I was hours away from death until the fluid was drained and I was out of danger. I needed a lot of time to recover, but there were several other reasons why I didn't go back to university. Not long after I was fully recovered, one of my doctors arranged for me to stay at a facility in Owen Sound where I would live for a few weeks and receive intense physio and occupational therapy. The occupational therapist was the most helpful as he showed me assistive devices that would help me better perform activities of daily living like dressing and hygiene independently.

My amazing doctors were trying everything they could to counteract the chronic effects from the Gang that were taking over my body. I'm not sure if it was one of my doctors or a physiotherapist who told us about a treatment that was even stranger than the ultraviolet skin frying and drying. This treatment was aimed at detoxifying the body and loosening up tight tendons and joints. Maybe there was a line in my palm or a glow around me that revealed a former life as a nudist because one also needed to be nudie-patootie during this procedure. I tried it because it could be done at home and there were no risks aside from it not working—which it didn't, but I'll tell you about it anyway.

Have you ever seen hilarious scenes in a movie where one of the actors tries to lose weight by getting naked and wrapping herself in cellophane? This procedure wasn't much different. I was nude and wrapped up like a cocoon from neck to toe, first in plastic, then in blankets. Next, I was helped onto a bed where I was to lie for about an hour while my body sweated out all of the toxins and loosened up my tendons and joints. I guess some of the thinking behind this procedure makes sense and perhaps it has helped a lot of people. However, it wasn't for me.

Major Switches

I had to think long and hard before returning to university in the fall of 1994. My worsening mobility was an issue, but something also had to change with my major. I liked science, especially anything to do with human physiology, but subjects like physics and chemistry baffled me. I knew I had to turn back to my English strengths.

I'd attended Mike's graduation ceremony with my parents and his girlfriend three months earlier in June. As I was leafing through the program, my eyes perked up when I spotted English majors who were graduating with a degree in rhetoric and professional writing. I'd never heard of that one before, and it intrigued me because I both loved and excelled at writing.

After much thought and soul-searching, I switched my major to English. I'd already started university a year late and then had another year's delay, so if I wanted to graduate in my twenties, I'd have to skip the co-op option. I would be able to carry over all of my health studies courses as electives, and if I stayed for an extra summer semester, I would finish in June of 1997.

This was a great move as I wasn't struggling to get good marks even though the courses were challenging. I ended up graduating, as planned, with an honours degree, but I had limited ideas as to what I was going to do with it. I had woulda, coulda, shoulda thoughts every time I recalled peers with the same major telling me about how they were going to enrol in extra courses to qualify for a post-graduate program to become speech therapists. Science courses were part of the curriculum, but no physics or chemistry. The bulk of the courses were in subjects I was interested or excelled in, like linguistics (love me some grammar).

So one issue was resolved, which freed me to move on to the next: my deteriorating mobility. Student residence was my best bet to be closest to the buildings where my classes were held. Although they were still a brisk hike from the residence, I was grateful that the majority of my classes were relatively close to each other. Enter Student Accessibility Services (SAS), that place over the rainbow with programs that give "flight" to happy little students. My mom and I met with an amazing woman three weeks before third year who told us all about the programs offered to break down barriers to a full and successful education experience for students with disabilities.

That visit was the first time I started associating myself with the word "disability." I don't balk nearly as much at the idea of wearing that badge now, but it was much more difficult to accept back then. It boosted my confidence when a senior student volunteer was with me to help with things like navigating exercise equipment at the gym or walking with me to classes on days when there was a lot of snow and ice on the pathways.

The SAS van was both my best and worst friend. The worst part was, of course, pride-related. At first, although challenging, I could climb the high, steep steps into the van, but by the second semester, the electronic lift was my ride up (I could still get down the steps safely). Unlike wheelchair users, I had to stand up on the lift, and I felt like I was on display while I was loaded up during high traffic times on campus. The best part (that superseded the mostly irrelevant worst part) was how I could easily schedule pickups to take me from residence to classes and between classes that were on opposite sides of campus. The van saved me a lot of time, although I tried to walk as much as I could. In important ways, then, what often seemed to be the worst of times had wonderful moments of, if not the best of times, certainly much better than worst.

CHAPTER ELEVEN:
EUROPEAN VACATIONS

Roses among the Thorns

I hope that you now better understand why I included my "worst of times" during my life with The Big C in the previous chapter. The bad times were often tempered with rich life experiences, like when I had the opportunity to tour Europe.

Mike spent two semesters at a UW sister university in Mannheim, Germany, in 1991. He was majoring in geography with a minor in German, and he jumped at the opportunity to go. Several days before he left, I was starting to get a lot of headaches that increased in severity each day. About two or three days after he left, HWMNBN showed up and started a love affair with Dr. P. A year or so later, the Gang got jealous and joined in on an acute level. This lurid love triangle started going to town on both my face and body.

Early in 1992, my parents made me a kind and generous offer. They were planning a trip to visit Mike during his March break and then tour with him for three weeks through several European countries. Their offer was for me to accompany them. When they first told me about their plan, I was looking forward to having the place to myself while they were away, so the offer took me by surprise. Unlike Mike, I didn't immediately jump at the chance because I was sporting several BABUDEEP attributes— mainly Blemished, Distended and Enflamed-Eyed with Watery thrown in as a bonus. The Gang still hadn't gained its full superpowers, so my mobility was half decent.

Well, I ended up choosing opportunity over pride, and I'm proud and happy that I did. When God closes a door, He opens a window, as they say. Not long after my high school graduation ceremony, I confessed to my parents that I wanted to delay starting university until the fall of 1992. The initial plan was to start in the winter 1991 semester, and they were not pleased with my decision. They assumed my reasons were purely appearance-related. That was part of it, but there were several more. I didn't want to start university part way through the year when most first-year students would be well established into their new university life. Plus, it would throw off my co-op schedule and delay taking some of the courses that had prerequisites. Most importantly, I just needed more time before taking on another huge life-changing experience.

Not starting university as initially planned opened a window for me to travel to Europe and have an unforgettable experience with my family. You may be getting weary of all the "God-talk" in this book, but I believe that God was the puppet master behind this story. He knew that HWMNBN would make an appearance less than a month after the fall 1991 semester started and that its negative effects, coupled with those of Dr. P and the Gang, would make it very difficult, if not impossible, for me to start university in the winter 1991 semester. The European vacation was the "window opening," and God flung it wide open.

Wanderlust

Before I get to the "window-opening" European vacation of '92, I'll start with tales of my earliest travels. I don't recall a summer when my family didn't travel somewhere within Ontario, Canada, the United States and on rare occasions, abroad. One of my first memories is travelling to Vancouver in a rented tent trailer in 1978. My only recollections are riding a huge tortoise at Stanley Park and wetting my camper bed, which I tried to cover up by laying my mom's hoodie over it.

I have vivid memories of the following summer when we took a four-week trip to England, Wales and Scotland. My grandma on my dad's side joined us, which worked out well because my parents could share a room with my brothers and I could share a room with her. Most of our rooms were at B&Bs, and in 1979, these rooms were almost closet-sized, included a shared bathroom and were thick with cigarette smoke. Not that a seven-year-old cared.

I've gotta give my dad huge credit for navigating around Great Britain on the wrong side of the car and road. Our rented hatchback was a five-seater. Seatbelts weren't required back then, so my dad cleared a space in the back between the suitcases—the best seat in the house for us kids. Roundabouts were a huge blessing. We started counting how many times my poor dad had to pull a "uey"—a U-turn—when he lost his way. We saw many of the main city and rural sites: Stonehenge was a highlight, although visitors could no longer climb on the ancient rocks. At least it wasn't fenced off like it is today.

Underage Drinking

We stayed at Miss Tickle's B&B, nestled in the Scottish moors. That was where I had my first ride on the booze cruise. Who would have thought it would involve ginger beer? I soon found out that there are two types of people in this world. There are those who like their ginger beer sweet, subtle and unassuming (the kind with 0.5 per cent alcohol that I'd tried and really liked earlier in the trip). Then there's the Miss Tickle-type: people who like their ginger beer to kick them hard in the back of the throat. I certainly felt a kick when I took a big gulp, hesitated for a moment and then swallowed it to be polite. My mom was less than pleased to see her seven-year-old daughter with a bit of a buzz.

Boys Will Be Boys

I hope my brothers don't mind my sharing the next two stories from this vacation, because they're the main players. The first story took place on one of the few days when my dad booked us into a hotel. When we arrived, my dad sent Ted to let people know we had arrived. Seconds later, we heard a terrified voice yelling, "Help! Help!" and saw Ted running past our car at warp speed followed by two big black dogs. Mike and I started laughing like hyenas. My mom admits that she was also laughing at the scene that looked like it was straight off a cartoon clip. In the end, the dogs backed off and the damage was limited to a small nip on one of Ted's heels.

Later, we took a bus to visit St. Giles' Cathedral, the historic parish church of Edinburgh. When we arrived, the bus driver was serious when he told passengers to be back on the bus on time and that anyone who was late would be left behind. Towards the end of the tour, Mike said he wanted to buy something at the gift shop and promised he'd meet up with us at the bus. There was still plenty of time before the bus was leaving, so my dad gave the OK. Little did Mike know that the cathedral had two main entrances, and when he opened the door at the wrong entrance, there was no bus. Obviously, he had listened closely to the bus driver's warning, and the poor kid started bawling, convinced he had been left behind. We were all waiting at the bus, and when Mike didn't show up, my dad headed back to the cathedral to find him. I don't think he even reached the entrance before he heard Mike's fearful cries echoing off of the sky-high ceilings. I wish I had been there to see Mike's look of utter relief when he saw my dad running towards him.

Cliffhangers

To cap off our British adventure, we went to the White Cliffs of Dover—you know, the place where there'll be bluebirds over? Ted, my dad and I crawled up and peeped over the White Cliffs of Dover, and my mom had a word or two to say to my dad afterwards—she was not pleased that he allowed his young children to lay down flat on their stomachs at the edge of a three-hundred-foot cliff. I have vague memories of chalky, white cliffs, blue waters below and a lot of birds. No fear whatsoever.

Six Countries in Under Three Weeks

OK, back to the window-opening European vacation. We flew to Frankfurt, Germany, and Mike met us at the airport. After we picked up our rental car, we drove to the hotel to get Mom and Dad settled, and then on to Mike's university residence where I would stay for the night. My parents would pick us up the next day to begin our European vacation. In addition to touring Germany, stops would include Austria, France, Belgium, Hungary and Holland.

Castles, Cars & Clocks

We were pretty jet-lagged when we arrived, but we tried to stay awake as long as possible to get used to the time change. Our first stop was Heidelberg, and I remember visiting the schloss (castle) ruins that rose high above the city. Known as the Red Walled Castle because it was constructed of red sandstone, it was completed in 1214. The castle has been partially restored, and compared to many castles I've visited over my life, the rooms were modest in size and decor.

I don't recall much about our day in Stuttgart, known for its rich cultural heritage, aside from strolling along the historical streets. It is Germany's automotive capital, and if fancy cars are your thing, this is the place for you. The city is home to headquarters for both Mercedes-Benz and Porsche, and separate museums showcasing both brands top lists of the best things to see. If cars and wine are your thing, then the city and its lush countryside will be like heaven to you due to the numerous vineyards that stretch all the way to the city centre. I feel like I just wrote an ad promoting the city; maybe I should demand payment from the mayor.

Munich has sections that look like you've stepped into a 365-day-long Oktoberfest. Stereotypical German staples abound: bier, brot and bratwurst (beer, bread and—wouldn't cha know!—bratwurst is the same in English and German!). I never developed a taste for beer, but man, the bread and bratwurst were out of this world—melt in your mouth! In Marienplatz (St. Mary's Square), my favourite site was the glockenspiel located on the 278-foot tower of the neo-Gothic New City Hall, a building that dominates the square. I thought the cuckoo clock we had when I was a kid was cool, but this thing blew me away. Two levels with moving figures that play out scenes of the city's history—a royal wedding, a jousting tournament and a ritualistic dance. The grand finale is a golden bird emerging at the top of the clock and chirping three times. Throughout the performance, different tunes are played on the clock's forty-three bells, and they're super loud. I have to wonder if earplugs are part of the welcome package for those who work within earshot!

Our next stop was the grounds of Neuschwanstein Castle, a fairy-tale castle built atop a rock ledge in the Alps of Bavaria. As we were getting out of the car, we noticed a crowd of people forming and then rushing towards something. We were curious, so we joined the crowd. Turned out that Mikhail Gorbachev and his wife Raisa were also on the grounds and there was a helicopter nearby waiting to whisk them away. This was exciting because, as the final leader of the Soviet Union, Gorbachev had presided over the fall of communism and was the recipient of the 1990 Nobel Peace Prize. I wiggled my way through the crowd and got so close to the ex-leader that I could have reached out and touched him. I decided to avoid arrest and took a picture instead. My mom got almost as close to Raisa and said that the former first lady looked directly at her and smiled. I got another great picture of the helicopter taking off with the castle in the background, an appropriate scene for a fairy-tale castle.

The castle was commissioned by King Ludwig II of Bavaria, also known as The Fairy Tale King. Fun fact: Sleeping Beauty's castle at Disneyland is a copy of this one. Our tour guide told us Ludwig was more commonly known as Mad King Ludwig for being a zwutschkerl, a Bavarian phrase for someone who is a little bit of an idiot or not quite the sharpest tool in the shed. Luddy was an uber-perfectionist, which explains why construction that began in 1869 and was expected to be completed three years later was still incomplete in 1886, the year the king drowned himself. The castle remains incomplete to this day.

Movies, Moguls & Madness

After we entered Austria, my mom and I boarded a bus in Salzburg to take the "Original *Sound of Music* Tour" (I guess the "Unoriginal Tours" were all sold out). The tour was a little contrived, with the movie soundtrack playing on the bus, but we joined in when the driver encouraged everyone to sing along. There were stops at Basilika St. Michael, where the wedding scene was filmed, as well as the Pegasus Fountain and the steps where Maria and the brats sang "Do-Re-Mi." We saw the glass gazebo where fated lovers Liesl and Rolf danced around singing "Sixteen Going on Seventeen." The bus passed by the hill where the opening scene was filmed and the site that served as the back of von Trapp manor where the boat flipping scene was filmed. Fun fact: The back and front of the manor were two separate mansions.

Palaces, Prima Donnas & Painters

I was most excited to visit France, Paris actually. We stayed at a hotel in Versailles, a residential suburb of Paris. We visited the Palace of Versailles on our first day, and the grounds were incredible. The palace itself was impressive, although it started to turn into a big gold blur after a while.

King Louis the XIV, a.k.a. the Sun King (hence the gobs of gold in every nook and cranny), wanted to expand what was originally a simple two-storey hunting lodge into the greatest palace in the world. It reminded me of Mad King Ludwig, as he spent nearly fifty years expanding the palace. Possibly another zwutschkerl?

I was so excited the next day because we were taking the train to Paris. I hadn't slept that well because the hotel had thin walls, and, as they say, "The French are the best lovers." No matter, as soon as I got off the train, I started to drink in the atmosphere of this magical city. We saw all of the big sites: the Arc de Triomphe, Notre-Dame, the Louvre (Mona is a teeny, tiny chick), even the risqué Moulin Rouge (ooh la la). Unfortunately, we could only go up the first two tiers of the Eiffel Tower because the third tier was under construction—again, no matter. By the way, if you're ever in Paris, be sure to stop by a patisserie that sells lemon tarts—c'est magnifique!

I hope what I have to say next doesn't sour you on Paris. It definitely shouldn't because I think we were just unlucky enough to run into the rudest Parisians in Paris. I'm pretty sure there's only about six of them, and they literally looked down their noses at us, rolled their eyes and sighed in disgust when we tried to order something in French—pushy, impatient prima donnas and doms. Unfortunately, this took a little bit of magic out of the day.

We also visited a lesser-known art gallery (at least compared to the Louvre) called Musée de l'Orangerie. The museum showcases a wide array of impressionist art, including works by my favourite artist, Claude Monet. One of the rooms displays a huge painting of Monet's *Nympheas* (*Water Lilies*) that is wrapped around several walls. Taking photographs was forbidden, but everyone else was doing it, so I got out my camera. As I was aiming the lens, I got caught, but I snapped the picture just in time (this time, my actions justifiably ticked-off the Parisian).

Visiting Monet's home, now a museum, in the village of Giverny (about seventy-five kilometres from Paris) wasn't on the agenda, but we squeezed it in. Unfortunately, the museum was closed, but I could still lean over the fence and get a decent look at the spectacular grounds. The gift shop was open, and I bought some seeds from Monet's garden. I recently came across that seed packet, still unopened. The front of the packet is a copy of one of Monet's paintings, and it's now displayed on one of the walls in my apartment.

Dolls & Dutch Dudes

I won't go into any details on Belgium (we mainly toured Brussels), but Budapest, Hungary, was quite the place. Fun fact: Budapest is actually pronounced like there's an "h" between the last two letters—"pesht." Driving through the city, the harsh effects of communism were evident in several run-down areas. However, there were also many beautiful attractions like Buda Castle and St. Stephen's Basilica. And most things were super cheap; I could get a quality meal—drink, side, main course, dessert—for less than $2 (back in the days when the Canadian dollar was strong).

I also purchased my first matryoshka, or Russian wooden nesting doll, in Budapest. The doll was beautifully hand-painted in bright colours with exquisite details. I collect dolls, and they all have names; this doll became Mary. I paid a pretty penny for Mary, but she was worth much more. Twenty-six years later, Mary gained a BFF when I purchased another Russian doll in Russia (you'll soon read about that trip). Martha is a factory-made doll, not as pretty as Mary, but still cherished.

Holland, a.k.a. the Netherlands, was a favourite destination. It lived up to some of the stereotypes as there were tulips, bicycles and blondes everywhere. We only had a day to spend there, and while the popular choice might have been to head to Amsterdam, the capital city, we headed to a lesser-known city called Haarlem. When I heard the word Haarlem, all I could think about was the Harlem Globetrotters—the famous American exhibition basketball team. I didn't expect to see a bunch of tall, dark and handsome basketball players in Haarlem, but I did encounter a few tall, blonde and handsome Dutch dudes. But I digress.

Sobering Experiences

You may have heard of *The Hiding Place*, a book written by Holocaust survivor Corrie ten Boom and later adapted into a movie. The ten Booms lived in Haarlem and were not Jewish, but they were strong Christians. When the Nazis invaded Holland in 1940, the ten Boom family, knowing the high risks, partnered with the Dutch underground and hid Jewish families in their large home. Corrie's bedroom closet was renovated to create a secret room behind a false wall where these unfortunate folks could hide if there was a Nazi raid. The ten Booms were betrayed by a man who asked them to help his wife who he claimed had been arrested. This was a ruse, and Corrie, her sister Betsie and their elderly father Caspar were arrested, imprisoned and later sent to a concentration camp (Caspar and Betsie died in prison). Ironically, the Jewish people that were hiding in the secret room at the time of the arrest were never discovered. The ten Boom home was converted into a museum, and it was a sobering experience to walk through the home, hear details about Corrie and her family (many not included in the book), and see the hiding place that is now uncovered in Corrie's bedroom closet.

On our way back to Germany, we got a glimpse of what Corrie and her sister must have endured in the concentration camp. On an appropriately dismal and rainy day, we drove to the medieval town of Dachau to visit the Dachau Concentration Camp Memorial Site. The visit is still etched in my mind. The steel gates are imprinted with the words "ARBEIT MACHT FREI" (work sets you free). The crematorium ovens. The prisoner barracks were initially made to house two hundred, but they in fact housed two thousand. The site where train tracks once carried the trains that brought in thousands of innocent prisoners. The high fences laden with barbed wire. There were also many pictures of prisoners and guards mounted inside the buildings and on outdoor memorials. It was not a fun day, and it's not a visit for everyone, but it was a contemplative experience for me.

Six Countries in Under Two Weeks

It wouldn't be until twenty-six years after my tour with Mike and my parents in 1992 when I would return to Europe. In 2018, I took a once-in-a-lifetime twelve-night cruise on the Baltic Sea. Perhaps I had too many thoughts of *The Love Boat*, a show my parents wouldn't let us watch but we found ways to watch anyway, or the movie *The Poseidon Adventure* (the original version with Gene Hackman) in my head because this type of travelling wasn't exactly on my bucket list. As usual, Mike convinced me that it would be better to visit countries along the Baltic Sea via cruise than car. Better, but much more expensive. I was between jobs at the time, but my parents offered to pay, and I vowed that I'd pay them back some day.

My parents were already in England touring with friends when Mike and I flew to London in early June. They met us at the airport, and we hopped a train to Southampton where our cruise ship was docked (yep, that's the same place where fated passengers were loaded onto the *Titanic*). We looked forward to some shore days, some sea days and a plethora of great food and entertainment.

The first shore day was in Oslo, Norway. We took a bus tour to the Viking Ship Museum, home of three remarkably well-preserved longships. The *Oseberg* is the seventy-foot-long, sixteen-foot-wide centrepiece of the museum; it is the most complete Viking ship ever found. It was a pleasure yacht dating back to AD 800. The bow of the longship has the most amazingly carved head of a serpent, and the stern of the ship is carved as its tail. It could have been a replica of the sea monsters that people reported to have seen back in the day. Perhaps the pleasure of seamonster-watching was the Viking equivalent of today's whale-watching excursions.

The *Gokstad* was even larger at seventy-six feet long and seventeen feet wide. It was a trading longship that could seat up to seventy people. The ship was built to be more seaworthy than the *Oseberg,* allowing Vikings to venture into deeper and darker waters that set the perfect stage for Norse myths of encounters with even scarier monsters like the kraken, gigantic octopuses with bodies so big they could be mistaken for an island. The *Tune* is like the lesser-known and revered cousin of the first two longships. This ship is a fragment of its counterparts, as only a twenty-two-metre section of it was found. The remains were also in much poorer condition, but experts estimate that it was a courier ship built for twelve oarsmen. The *Tune* does have some cool stories behind it, including how it was initially thought to be a "grave ship" built for an important Viking. Not an outlandish story, though, due to the discovery of a burial chamber below the mast with the remains of a Viking man and his trusty steed.

A Bevy of Busts

From there, we moved on to Vigeland Park, the world's largest sculpture park made by a single artist (Gustav Vigeland). Most of the park's 212 bronze and granite sculptures take human form, and each one of these statues was sculpted "puris naturalibis" (in a state of nature)—naked as a jaybird (and mostly anatomically correct). These statues are all either human-sized or giant-sized. Some show people alone, others in pairs and groups. They're always active—walking, running, shaking a fist, embracing. The artist's intent was to depict a wide range of human experiences, so some are laughing, some are enraged, some are in love. The statues all have simple names like *Angry Boy*, one of the most well-known. My favourite, *Dancing Young Woman*, was a life-sized statue of a woman standing on one foot with her hands raised above her head and holding several snake-like strands of her long hair; she reminded me of Medusa. The park was a little odd, and a tourist review I read called it "weirdly beautiful." But I'm all for the strange and bizarre, and I highly recommend a visit.

Copenhagen, Denmark was the next shore day, and our bus tour included a harbour cruise. I was enamoured by the rainbow of brightly-coloured facades that lined a city neighbourhood along the route. We also saw *The Little Mermaid* statue, Denmark's most famous tourist attraction, however, it was a fair distance from the boat. I was excited when we got back on the bus and our driver said that we'd be stopping by the statue to see it up close. Of course, the statue was not inspired by the Disney movie, rather the Hans Christian Andersen fairy tale. The over one-hundred-year-old bronze and granite statue, which was smaller than I expected, shows the mermaid sitting on a rock in the harbour wistfully looking out over the water as her transformation from mermaid to human is almost complete. This is yet another nudie-patootie statue, and sculptor Edvard Eriksen used his wife as the nude model. Unfortunately, the statue has been vandalized several times since it was unveiled in 1913, including in 1961, when a bra and panties were painted on the mermaid and her hair was "dyed" red.

Medieval Times

Tallinn, Estonia was another destination, and we visited the city's legendary Old Town, one of the best preserved medieval towns in Northern Europe. Once you set foot on the cobblestones, it truly feels like you're back in the times of Guinevere and Sir Spam—I mean, Lancelot. The gothic town hall that towers over the main square was completed in 1404, and the weathervane that sits atop the spire has been standing guard since 1530. The Church of the Holy Ghost is certainly ghostly and is not only one of the oldest churches in Tallinn, it's undergone no changes since its completion at the end of the fourteenth century. The oldest clock in Tallinn is carved into one of the church's outside walls. The inscription on the clock reads, "I strike time correctly for all, for the maidservant and for the manservant, for the master and for the mistress of the house. No one can reproach me." Clearly, no one has.

Oh, Those Russians

Russia—St. Petersburg to be exact—was next, and it was like going through customs at the airport to get from the ship onto Russian territory. Our bright, bubbly bus tour guide named BB had a wealth of knowledge on anything related to the historic city. The ship was docked for two days, giving us time to see almost all of the major sites.

On the first day, we stopped several miles from the city to visit The Catherine Palace, built for Catherine I by her husband Peter the Great. When we first arrived, I was disappointed to see a huge line-up at the entrance. No matter, BB assembled the troops, led us through the crowd and into the palace where she talked us through each room, barely stopping to take a breath as she shared endless details. Soon it was lunchtime, and we drove to a place that was more like a banquet hall than a restaurant. There, we were served traditional Russian fare—you guessed it, borscht was on the menu. Like a good tourist, I tried it, but I gave the rest to Mike, who finished it.

After lunch we visited that colourful church with the onion-shaped domes and gold spires that I'd always associated with Russia. I didn't know much about Russian history, including the name of that famous church. When I heard the church's name, it sounded as over-the-top as its beautiful exterior and interior: the Church of the Savior on Spilled Blood. The name is a bit of a mouthful, but one of the names of St. Basil's Cathedral, the church in Moscow that often gets mixed up with the Spilled Blood church, is Cathedral of the Intercession of the Most Holy Theotokos on the Moat—now that's a mouthful.

Speaking of Russia's greatest love machine, we also visited Yusupov Palace, once home to Prince Felix Yusupov, part of a group of nobles allegedly involved in

Rasputin's death. The palace was the site of the death, but there are several versions of how this charismatic monk met his demise. One version pins Rasputin's death on his powerful influence over Russia's royal family, especially the queen, who believed he could heal her hemophiliac son. In the palace basement, there are rooms set up to re-enact the mystery-shrouded event from December 1916. One of the rooms displays a wax figure of Rasputin sitting at a dinner table with cakes and a wine glass in front of him, all laced with cyanide. In the other room, wax figures of the assassins are displayed in a huddle waiting for Rasputin to take the bait.

Tour guides said the poison didn't work, and when the assassins discovered that their plan was foiled, they shot the holy man several times and beat him with clubs. Barely alive, Rasputin somehow managed to make it out of palace and into the courtyard, but he was soon grabbed by the assassins, who drove to a bridge over the icy Nevka River and threw him in. Some say Rasputin then died of hypothermia. Other versions say that he died inside the palace after being shot three times, the third shot in the forehead at close range. I won't detail the remaining versions—I fear that if you're reading this close to bedtime, I may have already set you up for a nightmarish slumber.

Another highlight was the State Hermitage Museum, and I would encourage you to visit its website to take a virtual tour of this wondrous place. The ginormous museum includes a collection of more than three million works of art and artefacts from around the globe that are spread across 120 rooms. You'd need at least a full day, maybe two, to see everything, but we saw most of the star players, including Michelangelo's unfinished marble statue *Crouching Boy* (another nudie-patootie) and the *Kolyvan Vase*, which is the biggest piece of jasper in the world, weighing in at almost nineteen tons. We also went into the Leonardo da Vinci Room and were told that it tops the Louvre because it has not one but two of Leo's masterpieces—*Madonna Litta* and *Benois Madonna*. That's what BB told us, but Mona tops them both, at least in my mind.

Nature Calls Us to the Open Air

We were on another bus tour in Helsinki, Finland, when the driver slowed down as we drove past *Bad Bad Boy*, an 8.5 metre-high, 7.5-ton statue of a boy that's located in the city's west harbour. So why is the boy bad, you ask? Because he's buck naked and holding on to his ... "boyhood" with an *Uh oh, I just got caught* expression on his face while "watering" the pavement below. Initially, the statue was located on Helsinki's west harbour, where this naughty boy was positioned to take a permanent wee-wee into the Baltic Sea. Oh, those Fins!

We were then transported to a rural landscape from the olden days. Seurasaari Island Open-Air Museum was built in 1909 to showcase Finland's folk history, and it represents four centuries of rural life. Thirty-five buildings are sprawled around the museum grounds, including smoke cabins, crofts (small, enclosed plots of land adjoining a house), manors, a church and a renovated parsonage. All staff are dressed in garb that reflects the era, and they'll tell you about each area you visit—in English! There weren't many people there that day, so Mike and I got private tours of the places we visited. This allowed us to share personal information with the staff like where we were from and what we'd seen so far. It was a bit of a walk to the museum, and along the way we met up with some Canadian friends who had also stopped by the museum on vacation—a flock of Canada Geese.

Hypnotic Events

Fun wasn't restricted to shore days; the activity calendar was filled with entertainment throughout. There was a small skating rink on the bottom level of the ship, and the show was fantastic—the professional skaters were as good as any I've seen live or on TV. There was also a talented magician who mystified us with his illusions. Several times, staff got together for a theme night and would dress up and sing and dance with the passengers. One night was a seventies theme. I wanted to dress up to reflect the era, and a tie-dyed top and a bunch of flashy jewelry sufficed. When *YMCA* came on, a bunch of male staff appeared dressed like members of the Village People. They started bumpin' and grindin' on the female passengers, including me, but it was all in fun. The hunky dude who pulled me aside was topless (fine with me), so he was probably representing the Native American.

My favourite entertainer was a hypnotist (I'll call him Dick) who blew us away. Dick managed to get this big strong guy (I'll call him Tom) under his spell, convincing him that his name was Sally. Dick also convinced Tom to get angry when someone called him by his real name. It was beautiful, and we would bust a gut every time Dick clapped his hands to put Tom under his spell and then call him Tom. Tom got increasingly angry, insisting that his name was Sally. When Dick clapped him back into reality for the last time, Tom said he didn't remember a thing. We were sitting near Tom, and when he returned to his seat, I saw him turn to his wife and ask her what Dick made him do. Before she had time to explain, Dick took one more shot at the poor dude, clapping his hands and calling him Tom, which made him super angry again—hysterical!

Fifteen Minutes of Fame

Lastly, I thought you might be interested in reading about the times when Mike and I were the entertainment! Actually, it's more accurate to say that Mike was a three-time entertainer. One sea day when Mike and I were at a bar, a staff member announced that a karaoke machine was being set up for anyone to use. I'd always wanted to try karaoke, but I couldn't bring myself to do it. Mike was braver than me, and after looking through the song selections, he got up and belted out a fine rendition of "I Melt with You" by the eighties band Modern English.

    The opportunity arose again when Mike and I were at a lounge that held smaller events like the trivia challenge our family crushed. We had read in the activities calendar that there was a karaoke competition being held in the lounge over two nights, with finalists performing on the grand stage two nights later. This was the second night of the competition, and we were there to see the contestants (at least I was). Before the competition started, the MC announced that anyone was welcome to sign up, and Mike turned to me with a *What do you think?* expression on his face. This was a much bigger crowd than the other day at the bar, and there was no way I was going to do it. Yeah, I know, those words are soon followed by how Mike's mystical powers got me to change my mind. This time was no different. I caved like a house of cards, and Mike signed us up and grabbed a list of song options. We settled on "Video Killed the Radio Star" by The Buggles—Mike singing the lyrics and me doing the "Ooh wa oohs."

    I was terrified when I stepped on stage and the MC announced our brother and sister act. When the music started, I focused my gaze above the audiences heads to help calm my anxiety. This worked, and before long I was movin' and groovin' to the music and exaggerating the "Ooh wa oohs." We received roaring applause. Most of the other competitors had practiced their songs, and many of them were pretty good, so we were so surprised when we were nominated as one of the six acts to move on to the finals at the big stage in the ginormous auditorium.

The thought of performing on a stage that might as well be London's Royal Albert Hall nauseated me. Mike sensed this and kindly offered to perform a different song without me. The finals were still two days away and there was a shore day in between. I managed to put the competition out of my mind during the day, but it plagued me when we returned from our tour in the late afternoon. Mike and I won as a team, and I wasn't even sure if they'd let him perform by himself. I'd dealt with and defeated evil stomach butterflies before, so I shooed them away and told Mike that I'd perform.

The competition was the next day, so we needed to practice. We thought about doing the same song but then decided on a new one. Needless to say, it was another eighties era song (I'm an eighties gal through and through), but this time we would share the lyrics. Ever heard of the eighties band Human League? There is a male and a female lead singers, and we chose the song "Don't You Want Me"—the one with the chorus, "Don't you want me baby? Don't you want me oh, oh, oh, oh?"

The night of the competition arrived. This time our parents would be in the audience, but I didn't bother looking for them because the auditorium was full. I think we were third or fourth in the line-up, and only one of the judges that were chosen from the audience seemed to be taking the competition seriously. Maybe too seriously, as he raked one poor young girl over the coals for her rendition of "Hallelujah" by Leonard Cohen. True, she was awful, but not many professional singers can do justice to that song and I thought she was courageous for trying. My anxiety-calming technique of looking above the audience wasn't necessary this time because I could hardly see a thing through the bright stage lights. We pulled it off again. The audience and the judges were kind, but we didn't win (not that we expected to).

A Capital Day

After we disembarked from the ship, we took a train back to London. Our flights home were booked for the next morning, so we had the rest of the day to tour the city. We decided to take an open-air, hop-on hop-off bus tour where we saw many of the most popular tourist attractions. We got off at the gates of Buckingham Palace, and I was reminded of *National Lampoon's European Vacation*. I still roll over with laughter every time I think of a number of scenes of the visit to London.

Well, that's about it for highlights of my "best of times" related to travel. I won't go into as much detail on the following life experiences—the chapter is already way too long! I'm just going to write a few more paragraphs related to grade school, pets and jobs and the role they've played in making my life full and fulfilling.

CHAPTER TWELVE:
SCHOOL DAZE

Performance Reviews

I was as active in school as I was with the 2nd Avenue Gang. I mentioned earlier that I was a bossy kid, which was reflected in several of my junior school report cards. In nursery school, I remember having to sit on the stage, the place where naughty children were sent. My crimes were usually for being Miss Bossypants or for being smart-mouthed with the teachers. I wasn't a "problem child"—I rarely smart-mouthed (especially after my dad found out about my rude behaviour), and my bossypants were more of a light cotton blend than a heavy denim.

I think that I mainly just wanted attention, so that stage eventually became a place where I could be applauded for my theatrics instead of punished for them. When the teachers announced that we would be doing the play *Little Red Riding Hood*, my ears perked up. I thought I'd be perfect for the role of the Big Bad Wolf—after all, I had displayed bad behaviour and I was one of the biggest kids in the class. But it was not to be, and the two starring roles went to other kids. I did get a role: Red's mom. Seriously?

Does the mother even appear in the story? I think Red just says, "Bye Mom!" as she heads off on her merry way. I made the most of my fifteen seconds on stage and hoped that my next stage appearance would be longer.

It was a while before I appeared in my next stage performance, and this time I wasn't acting in a play. Part of the elementary school curriculum included writing and presenting a speech to the teacher and my classmates. My brothers and I wrote our speeches by ourselves, and my dad always helped us finesse them. In Grade 7, I wrote a funny speech about my pet rabbits and their amazing procreation skills, and I made it to the big stage in the school gym. I got second place in the Grades 7 and 8 division, which meant I would move on to the local legion. I was really on my game and took first place this time.

The next step was at a Legion in another small town, but this time I froze as soon as I got on stage. I still remember that feeling of absolute horror and embarrassment as I looked out on the crowd and tried desperately to remember my speech. The words eventually came to me, but I just zipped through the speech, void of any flair, and sat down with my head hung low.

I was back on the stage in Grade 8, this time with a decent role as Elsa von Schrader, the snooty baroness who schemed to keep Maria and Georg apart, in *The Sound of Music*. Opening day was set for mid-May, so I'll give you a moment to do the math on that.

Opening day in mid-May.

Big C diagnosis in mid-March.

Yep, no play for me. This was disappointing, but there were three more opportunities to come in high school. I was never the star, perhaps because they were all musicals. I can carry a tune, but there were some excellent singers among my peers.

In Grade 9, we did *Grease*, but I was never on stage. My part was merely as page turner for one of the piano players. Not much, but I got to attend the rehearsals and I enjoyed watching my peers in action.

In Grade 10, we did *Anne of Green Gables*, and I got a decent part as Mrs. Spencer, the woman who made the mistake of bringing Anne home instead of a boy. If you think about it, without Mrs. Spencer there would be no Anne, so maybe I was the star after all (in my head).

Little Shop of Horrors was in Grade 12, and I had some decent roles, nothing of note, but they kept me on the stage quite a bit.

Come Blow Your Horn

Plays and musicals weren't my only opportunities to take the stage during my school years. In Grade 6, my best friend Shawn and I took up trumpet, and our small elementary school band played during assemblies. They were on the gym floor, not the stage, but hey, work with me here!

The stage performances came in high school when I joined the concert band. I always wanted to play French horn, but the only brass instruments offered in elementary school were trumpets and trombones. I grabbed the chance to play French horn in high school and so did a good friend of mine. We felt kinda special because from Grades 10 to 12, we were the only horns of the French persuasion in the band.

A new music teacher who was big on competitions arrived in Grade 11. We practiced more frequently as he prepared us for our first big competitions, which were divided up amongst several Ontario locations. We won our division.

Concert band was fun, but jazz band was a blast. French horns consider themselves above the jazz scene, so I switched to trombone. Playing two other brass instruments helped me slide into the role (not punny!), and it didn't take long for me to become a decent trombonist. This time, the music teacher had bigger plans. We would start with a small competition in our Ontario district, and if we won, we'd be flying to a big competition in Winnipeg. We were really good, if I do say so myself, and we even came up with a name for our band: Hoover's Groovers, named after our cherished leader. We even got new outfits that made us look like a rainbow. We dominated the Ontario competition and did well in Winnipeg, but no trophies to take home this time. No matter, we had fun both at the competition and during our free time when Hoover let us run wild on the prairie land.

On the Ball

That wasn't the only time I ran wild during my school years (not a bad segue, huh?), as I played my share of sports. Softball was a favourite, and while I wasn't the fastest runner, I could drive that ball hard and straight, which usually got me to at least second base (sometimes all the way home). In Grade 10, I remember a boys against girls softball game during gym class when I unintentionally drove a ball straight at the pitcher and got him pretty good in the arm. I felt terrible, but some of the guys came up to me after the game, and one of them said, "Wow, you're a good hitter!"

Basketball was another favourite, and my height was a bonus. In elementary school you could only be on official school teams (official meaning team members had to wear itchy polyester uniforms in ugly school colours) in Grades

7 and 8. I joined girls' basketball in Grade 7, and we were a force to be reckoned with. I wasn't even close to the strongest player, but I held my own and we almost won the elementary school district championship one year.

Interestingly, the championship that year was held at the high school where Mike was in Grade 9 and Ted was in Grade 12. Ted and his friends were referees, and one of his friends refereed the final game. Our coach and team were furious with him for missing a clear foul when a player from another team pushed one of our players. She lost her balance and fell to the ground. Ironically, the player that was pushed to the ground ended up marrying this referee less than a decade later—great story for the grandkids.

My favourite sport of all was field hockey, that vicious sport with good reason to require mouth and shin guards. I started playing in Grade 8, but my Big C diagnosis kept me from playing in Grade 9. I'm not sure why I waited until Grade 12 to resume playing—probably that pesky pride of mine. I was the team captain in Grades 12 and 13, not because I was the best player, but because I was the only one to step up. Again, I wasn't the fastest, but I was strong, and right fullback was the perfect position for me because I could drive that hard plastic ball from one side of the field to the other. Like every high school team, we were the Royals, and our colours were purple and gold. This time we had kilts—purple polyester skirts we'd wrap around our waists and secure with Velcro. We felt very official in our uniforms, and although we practiced a lot and tried hard, we were the worst team in our division of three high schools.

But boy did we have fun.

Our goalie was the best player on our team. She was only in Grade 10, but she had a lot of previous experience with the sport outside of school. You'd think we'd have won more than one game per season with a goalie like that, but it definitely wasn't her fault. The scores were usually 1-0, and it's amazing that she saved so many shots. She also had a great sense of humour, and we became good friends and clowned around a lot. She was the one responsible for our team's "fight song." At the beginning of each game, the opposing team and anyone within earshot was baffled when they heard us shout at the top of our lungs:

U, G, L, Y – you ain't got no alibi
You ugly, you ugly, your moma says you ugly
M, O, M, A – how do you think you got that way
Your moma, your moma, your moma's ugly too
Gooooo Royals!

As I think about it now, part of the reason why opponents were baffled is that our chant was a little derogatory towards a family icon. Personally, I'd had a very positive experience with my own mother and even some experience with being a mother myself, although not in the traditional sense. Let me tell you about it.

CHAPTER THIRTEEN:
ANIMANIAC

Animal House

I've never been a baby momma, but I've had the honour of being a pet momma multiple times (I'm on a roll with these segues, baby!). I mentioned that time when I yanked a poor cat's tail to try and get its attention and ended up looking like Freddy Krueger. This isn't an excuse for my cruel actions, but my intentions were innocent. I wasn't allowed to get a cat, and I just wanted to shower that cat with love as I held and cuddled it. I'm an animal lover to the core, and thanks to my parents who, although on a slightly smaller scale, also love animals, this affection was indulged throughout my childhood and teenage years.

Not Your Average Vermin

Rodents seem to be the pets of choice for many young kids, especially their first pet. You may argue that puppies and kittens take centre stage as the chosen ones, but they're usually family pets whereas I'm talking about a pet that was exclusively mine—and exclusively my responsibility.

My first pet was a gerbil I got for Christmas when I was seven. This was also the Christmas when I stopped believing in Santa Claus. During my family's annual get-everything-purchased-in-one-day Christmas shopping extravaganza, I sat on Santa's lap at a Costco-esque store with an enormous toy section (largest in Ontario at the time) and told him that I wanted a gerbil for Christmas. I don't know where they found this dream-crushing imposter, but he told me that Santa doesn't give pets for Christmas. I hope he got a lump of coal in his stocking that year!

I named my gerbil Cuddles (barf, I know), and she was actually quite friendly for a gerbil. I remember riding my bike around with her on my shoulder. I used to frequent the Children's Library, and the librarian was more than happy to let me in when I had Cuddles with me. All the kids would gather around me to have a look and ask if they could hold her. My mom wasn't too happy about Cuddles' frequent residency on my shoulders. Like all rodents, gerbils are natural chewers, and several holes kept showing up on my T-shirts.

She was even less happy the day Cuddles got out of her cage when I wasn't around and somehow made it down the long, wooden staircase. From there, she proceeded into the living room where my mom was entertaining a bunch of ladies. My mom later told me that the first woman to spot the cheeky critter just raised her legs to keep Cuddles from climbing onto her lap. But it wasn't long before the other ladies spotted her. There wasn't any loud screaming, just some muffled shrieks and scrambling to leave the room while my mom yelled at me to come retrieve the intruder.

Cuddles met an unfortunate and untimely death one day, and I'll never forget it. I was allowed to let her run free in our family room because it had a door that could be closed to keep her from escaping into the kitchen or other rooms. It was almost suppertime, so I got up off the couch to search for her. When I spotted her, I got down on bended knee, and as I leaned over to grab her, she switched course and ran under my knee. What happened next was what Ted called "an atomic knee drop" that landed right on top of Cuddles. She made some strange twisty-twirly movements and then lay motionless on the floor. I sobbed through dinner and for the rest of the night, feeling like a murderer and vowing that I would never own a pet again.

Kids get over things quickly, and less than a year later, I adopted two more gerbils. I thought it would be nice to get two gerbils to keep each other company, and I named them Lozzie and Harry. Such unusual names—let me explain. Mike received the home edition of the Family Feud game for Christmas one year. Our family liked to watch the show together, and we all knew that Mike's quick wit and amazing sense of humour would make him the perfect host whenever we played. The questions were often over my head, and one time when he thought no one was looking, my dad whispered the answer to one of the questions in my ear. The question was related to Ozzie and Harriet Nelson. For you non-Zoomers out there, they starred in *The Adventures of Ozzie and Harriet*, an American sitcom that aired in the fifties and sixties. Anyway, the words I heard my dad whisper were, "Lozzie and Harry," so when I gave this answer, everyone knew the jig was up; my dad was cheating (again).

I entered the rat race when I was in high school, and these cuties were the best vermin I ever owned. I adopted my first rat at a pet store where I worked (more on that soon). He must have been male, but not just because I named him Reggie. Male rats are said to be especially cuddly and will often fall asleep while you're holding them or when they're resting on your lap, just like Reggie. Unlike my gerbils and rabbits, Reggie wanted to be with me most of the time, and it was easy to get him to come back to me when he wandered away.

Female rats are the active ones, and they love to wrestle with and chase other females. Over three decades after Reggie passed, I adopted two female rats instead of one so they would always have someone to play with. Females are also fighters, and sometimes playful wrestling turns into a loud fight. I've broken up many a girl fight after hearing shrill squeaking noises and finding the girls scratching, biting and pushing each other down. Worse, females are prone to mammary tumours that grow very fast and will continue to grow to sizes even larger than their own bodies if left untreated. Rats generally have short lifespans—two to three years—in comparison to gerbils, which can live up to four years (like Lozzie and Harry did). However, the short times I had with my rats (I adopted two more female rats after the others passed) were much more fun and fulfilling than those with my other rodent pets.

Wascally Wabbits

I think I was in Grade 4 when I heard about a man from our church who sold rabbits. I begged and pleaded with my dad to let me get one. He relented and even built a hutch, although it was to stay in the garage, not my room. I ended up with two giant albino rabbits that I named Coconut and Vanilla. These rabbits weren't quite as friendly as my gerbils. I pretty much had to yank them out of their cage, and they didn't respond well when I tried to cuddle them. They were fat, but they were also fast, and when they got away from me, it took several people to corner and catch them.

When they passed, I moved on to male and female dwarf rabbits that I named Boober and Cookie. They were pets, but my plan was to breed them and make some money. I think Cookie was pregnant about five seconds after I put them in a cage together, and then again about two seconds after they were reunited. At one point, I had about twenty-four bunnies on my hands, which was the topic of the winning speech I wrote about earlier. I ended up keeping two of the offspring and selling the rest.

I only named the ones that took a long time to sell, and one of them became Meanie because she made this strange growling sound and lashed out at me when I tried to pick her up. One day when a family stopped by to look at the remaining rabbits, my dad told me to call her Happy instead of Meanie, but there was no need. Miraculously, Meanie didn't growl or lash out when a young child said he wanted "That one" and picked her up. I didn't think Meanie would ever find a home, so I guess her problem was with me.

Going to the Dogs

We always had a family dog. Taffy was the favourite of everyone but me. She would have been considered an older dog when I was a little kid, and she didn't have much time for my efforts to get her to do what I wanted. She loved Ted, and as I wrote earlier, they played hockey together (hence the "wonder dog" moniker). Taffy lived to be seventeen (119 in dog years), and when she died of congestive heart failure, I was just as sad as anyone because she had warmed up to me as I grew older.

We didn't get another dog until I was in Grade 10, and what a dog she was. Maggie was also a Border collie, black lab cross, but while Taffy was mostly Border collie, Maggie was mostly black lab. Maggie was as sweet as could be to everyone when we first brought her home; however, when she was no longer a pup, her sweetness was confined to our family and a small handful of others.

I guess we should have noticed by the size of her paws that Maggie was going to be a big dog. In my dad's eyes, big dogs were outside dogs, and Maggie was literally in the doghouse (inside our dilapidated garage) before she was fully grown. We couldn't let her run around free, but the long length of rope tied to her collar still allowed her to roam around much of our large backyard.

Shawn was one of Maggie's small number of friends, and he looked after her whenever we went away. Sometimes younger kids in the neighbourhood would follow him when he went to feed her. The little stinkers knew how long Maggie's rope was, and they would stop about three feet shy of the rope's end and tease her. We later found out that a family we knew had adopted one of Maggie's siblings, but they soon returned it due to its bad temperament. This helped explain Maggie's intolerance of most people.

However, no animal responds well to teasing, and one day, one of the teasers roamed onto our property on his own. He misjudged the length of Maggie's rope, and she was able to reach him. Maggie's next actions proved that she wasn't a vicious attack dog. Although the kid ended up on the ground, Maggie could push all 140 lb. of me down when she got excited, so it likely just took a slight push to get the 80 lb. kid down. A big bruise formed on the kid's stomach from Maggie's small nip. Regardless, his parents couldn't do anything about it because he was trespassing and Maggie was tied up.

Casey came along during my last year of university, almost a decade after we'd moved to rural Shelburne. He was our first male dog, and he came to live with us out of a broken marriage where neither side could look after him. Their loss was our gain, as Casey was the most affectionate, and affection-seeking, dog we ever had. He was also a Border collie, black lab cross. Like Maggie, he was more black lab, but only in the structure of his head, nose and ears. He was actually quite awkward looking—small, thin legs on a thick, fleshy body.

We didn't care, he was such an obedient dog and a great companion. He was also smart. I wanted to teach him how to beg, and I thought it would take a long time; however, after less than a week of training, he would sit up straight on his bum with his bent paws at his chest when I made the "beg" motion. It was the cutest thing. Casey and Maggie had much shorter lives than Taffy, and they exhibited similar behaviours before the vet suggested that we put them down—constant panting, always restless, wandering around aimlessly.

Hold Your Horses

I wasn't thrilled at the thought of moving from what I still refer to today as our "real" home on 2nd Avenue West to rural Shelburne. I could walk to my high school in two minutes, but after the move I had to catch a bus that would take over twenty-two times longer.

I am passionate about horses. Whenever we came across a place that offered trail rides, I would beg my parents to stop. I also went to two different summer camps over five summers that offered horseback riding. Three of those years were at the camp where I learned and fell in love with English riding. I also learned how to jump, and I experienced a natural high every time I led my horse over the fences.

The property my parents wanted to move to had a garage with a stall built into it, and there were no health risks from car fumes because it was used only for storage. Any concerns I had about moving leapt out the window to their death when my dad told me I could get a horse. He sprang the horse surprise on me quite a while before we'd be moving, but I didn't have to wait that long. One of my mom's close friends lived on a farm that was close to the property. They had cows, but there was a small, separate paddock connected to an area in the barn that could shelter a horse, and the friend was more than willing to board my horse until it was time for us to move.

I ended up purchasing a two-year-old registered Quarter Horse mare named April Starfly. April was a beauty—chestnut-coloured with a white star and blaze from forehead to muzzle, plus cute white "socks" on three of her strong, slender legs. She was a good size, standing over 15 hands high, but she didn't come ready to ride. I was actually cautioned not to buy this horse by a family friend who would invite me over every now and then to ride his horses. There was nothing wrong with April health-wise, he just thought that I should get an older horse that was riding-ready.

In the end, he was right. University was less than three years away, and the many months spent training a young horse would have been better spent bonding with and safely riding an older, well-trained horse. The same friend who was temporarily boarding April knew of a woman who could help me train her. April was antsy and resistive of having a rider on her back, and even at the end of training, keeping her under control remained a challenge. I loved riding fast on a horse, and April loved to run. Fun fact: Quarter Horses own the record for the fastest horse at any distance, something I just learned about a month ago.

Anyway, yes, she loved to run, just not with someone on her back. Almost every time I would click my tongue and squeeze her belly to coax her into a run, she would start bucking after about two minutes and keep going until she bucked me off—ouch!

I ended up selling April earlier than planned because I just didn't have the skills to break a young strong-willed horse, and I was becoming increasingly frustrated. I never felt like we bonded the way I'd hoped, and I thought she'd be better off with more experienced owners, ideally ones who owned several horses.

It was a sad day when the new owners came to pick up April, but it was also scary—for about three seconds. I was having a last ride, and when I reached our long driveway, I motioned for her to speed up a little. We weren't going that fast, but when we approached the top of the driveway, she suddenly bucked me off. It was easy for her to do so because she'd never started bucking at that slow speed and I didn't feel the need to take a strong grip on the reins. After I fell, I started to move my legs but nothing happened. My young life flashed before my eyes during those three seconds before I got my legs moving and stood up.

I don't regret choosing April; it was fun watching her frolic around the fields, and I enjoyed learning how to train a horse. We also had many slow but pleasant rides together through the fields, and she was a great companion after I was plucked out of my beloved 2nd Avenue West neighborhood and placed into a quiet country environment. Selling April earlier than planned was a God-given blessing, as I was diagnosed for the second time around with The Big C a few months later. The last thing my family and I needed was the huge monkey wrench of selling a horse thrown into an already daunting situation.

I Wanna Iguana

There were several other pets, including lots of fish. My first fish was a black molly that I named Nel. When I started working at a pet store I got employee discounts, so I switched to tropical fish and had some beauties. Sometimes my bosses would take in sick or injured pets that needed one-on-one attention to nurse them back to health. Once they were well again, they could be sold. One day a sick iguana was dropped off and one of my bosses asked if I wanted to care for it. After a lot of convincing, my parents said I could, and I brought Lois home. I did what my boss recommended, but, unfortunately, Lois was gone after a couple of weeks.

CHAPTER FOURTEEN:
SHE WORKS HARD FOR THE MONEY

Filling Up My Piggy Bank

The pet store I mentioned was my first "real" job. Like many tweens, I started babysitting at the age of twelve, but although I was paid, I don't consider it to be my first real job. As an animal lover, I was ecstatic when I landed this dream job. It was the summer before Grade 10 when I was hired, and I worked on Saturdays after school started.

Twins in their twenties managed the store, and one of them was often mean to me, especially when her sister (who was really nice to me) wasn't around. I think she thought she was punishing me when she assigned me to do jobs that she didn't want to do herself, like cleaning out the poo-poo and pee-pee from the puppy and kitten pens. But I actually enjoyed it. Not the clean-up part, but I had to get the animals out of their pens to clean them, which gave me an opportunity to cuddle and play with them when she was busy with customers.

Right after that job ended, I started working at Burger Putt, a fast-food joint with mini-golf and a driving range. I loved that job—friendly, supportive managers and co-workers, and an all-around positive atmosphere. I loved driving the tractor that was equipped with an apparatus to pick up golf balls on the driving range. It seemed like the tractor was the preferred target when golf balls kept dinging off the cage built onto the tractor for protection.

We also served super-sized single, double and triple ice cream cones, to the delight of kids whose eyes widened as they said, "Wow, I've never had an ice cream cone this big before!" It also had those gaming tables where one person could sit at each end. One was the shoot 'em up, humans versus aliens video game Galaga. One dude used to stop by frequently with several rolls of quarters and play for hours. We liked to play, too, and there was a big competition to reach and retain high score.

The Friendly Café was my next stop, and it would be my last "teenage years" job before my Big C relapse. Another pair of sisters managed the café, but they were both friendly (lived up to the café's name) and kind to me. Customers were also kind, and the majority of them knew me or my parents, which is probably why I got great tips. Staff could eat for free, and I loved the chicken crepes—there was some kind of magic in the sauce. It was ironic that exactly one week before I became suspicious that The Big C may have returned, I was on my lunch break with a co-worker who remarked about how quickly I'd recovered the first time and how well I'd been doing since (*Twilight Zone* theme song in my head).

All Educated-Up with No Place to Go

My appearance-related pride wielded its ugly head again during my last year of university. I had no idea what to do with my degree, so I took both a Meyers-Briggs Type Indicator and a "job aptitude" test. When I received my test results, radio broadcasting was one the jobs in the "suitability" category. I debated writing about the primary reason why I thought this would be a good job for me as it still makes me cringe inside. Here it goes. The job sounded good because I would be behind a microphone and very few people would see me. I don't know why I was that insecure then. I'd been living with and adapting to the Gang-induced mobility losses for over four years, and I hadn't taken high doses of Dr. P for about the same amount of time. Although much finer and thinner, my hair was shoulder-length again/ and I was a healthy weight.

Anyway, there is a "window opening" to the story. I did enrol in and complete a post-graduate certificate program in radio broadcasting at a Toronto college. There, I discovered the many facets to a career in this area, including copywriting (commercials, news stories, public service announcements, etc.). I had strong written and communication skills, and I loved any kind of writing—my interest started to grow beyond hiding myself from the world.

While it was a huge blessing when a radio station hired me to work full-time as a copywriter with some production and on-air responsibilities, God creaked the window open a smidge before I got this job. While I was job searching, I had a lot of time on my hands, so I started volunteering at the nursing home where my mom worked as an RN. I was very close to my grandmas, who had both passed in 1991, so I thought spending time with the residents might help fill that void. It wasn't long before a spark was lit. I was so used to being the "patient" and having others care for me, so this was a chance to switch roles in a sense (although I never viewed the residents as "patients" and I wasn't their "nurse").

I was going to give radio broadcasting a chance, but deep inside, I felt that God was calling me to a different career, one that would fuel my growing passion to serve those who are often marginalized and overlooked in society. I left my copywriting job after one year and soon returned to college to earn two post-graduate certificates in gerontology multidiscipline and gerontology activation techniques. My goal was to become a programs director at a long-term care home, working with my staff to plan and implement meaningful individual and group programs and events to meet the needs and interests of residents with varying disability types. It wasn't long before I reached that goal, moving from part-time programs assistant to full-time programs director in less than a year. This was such a rewarding and fulfilling job, and I stayed at the home for over eight years until I started to realize that God had only partially opened the window. He had more plans for my career.

The year before I left that position, I'd heard about the Accessibility for Ontarians with Disabilities Act (AODA) that was enacted in 2005. My disability had pretty much reached a plateau, and it was my responsibility to stay active to keep from losing any more mobility. As a person with a disability, I had become uber-aware of physical access barriers. When I started researching the AODA more in depth, something inside me began to stir as I read about its principles of integration, dignity, independence and equity of opportunity, and its goal to make customer service, information and communications, employment, transportation, and the design of public spaces in Ontario accessible by 2025. I was back to college a few years later to complete a fourth post-graduate certificate in accessibility coordination. This is where I remained—window fully opened to the right career path—sometimes employed, sometimes searching, always learning.

I hope you've gotten a good taste of what a blessed life I've lived and why there's no need to feel sorry for me. Still not convinced? I live independently, work full-time and drive. I live pain-free (physically), and I've found peace to reduce pain of the emotional kind. My immediate family are all still with me, loving and supporting me through the best and worst of times. I'm a proud aunt to three beautiful nieces and a handsome nephew—all brilliant and pursuing independent lives away from the safety and familiarity of home. My two closest friends are like the sisters I never had, and we have a blast together.

Above all of this, I have a God and Saviour who loves me unconditionally and has been like a thread that has woven its way through the tapestry of my life. *Uh oh, I can almost hear you thinking, here comes the Bible-thumping chapter.* You caught me. This Jesus Freak is segueing into the final 3 chapters that will focus on God and His mercies throughout my journey with The Big C. I promise that it won't be preachy; this is my journey, not my sermon.

CHAPTER FIFTEEN:
TAPESTRY

Two-Sided Coin

Joyce Meyer often says that just like sitting in a garage doesn't make you a car, sitting in a church doesn't make you a Christian. I spent most of my teenage years and much of my adult life sitting in church. I wouldn't even say that I was a "Sunday Christian," as I just went to church, sang the hymns, sat through sermons (while anxiously looking at the clock), then returned home and resumed my "real" life.

Not that I didn't believe in God. I'd accepted Him into my heart at a young age. I vaguely remember that I stepped forward after an altar call when I was about nine. My parents believed that baptism was a personal choice to be made when someone is old enough to understand it and felt led to have it done, so I was dedicated, not baptized, as a baby. I was baptized in a pond when I was fifteen.

During my childhood and teenage years, I went to three different "churches." I had to put the word churches in quotes because the second one was the Murray Church

(MC), a formation of three families who met at our house on Sundays for a year or so. I was pretty young when the MC was in place, but I remember a lot of details and that I really enjoyed it. Talents within the families made for an experience that was church-like in every aspect but the building itself. We had piano, guitar, and banjo players, and real hymn books. While the adults stayed in the living room to listen to the fathers who took turns making sermons, we went to Sunday school in our family room; it was led in shifts by the mothers. There were seven kids and we were divided into the older kids (12+) and the younger kids. There were four others in their late teens/early twenties that attended but stayed in the living room for the sermons.

The MC was formed when the families decided to leave an Anglican church, but we all returned when a new pastor came on board. I had a good friend who was my age at that church and we had a lot of fun together. We both joined junior choir, and on Sundays we wore white robes and small wooden crosses around our necks that made us feel official. We even sat at the front of the church with the senior choir and took turns carrying a large cross on a pole, leading the procession of choirs and the pastor into the nave at the beginning of services.

We used to meet once a week for practices and enjoyed potluck dinners. I think I was in Grades 2 through 4 when we attended this church, and all my friend and I really cared about was establishing ourselves as the "cool kids." We poo-pooed most of the younger kids and only allowed those we deemed even remotely on our level to sit with us during dinner, let alone speak to us. The older kids ignored us, but most of the younger kids looked up to us (at least we thought so).

All of my childhood friends either didn't attend church or, like me, attended because our parents did. In Grade 4, one of the choir leaders announced that we were going to perform a musical and the subject was Jonah—you know, the one who was swallowed by a whale? Everyone had a part, but I don't recall what mine was. We performed at the church and some homes for the elderly, but I clearly remember when the leader announced that we would be performing at my elementary school.

I was "going out" with this guy who was new to the Shelburne area (to the envy of many Grade 4 girls), and there was no way that I was going to perform in front of him or the others in my circle of "coolest-in-the-school" friends. Even as a ten-year-old kid I was led by my foolish pride, and I was convinced that kids who "showcased" their faith were viewed as geeks. I bailed on the play, but my buddy didn't, and afterwards, everyone—including my friends and boyfriend—had a lot of praise for her and the choir's performance. So that's what? The fifth time I've written about a pride-related missed opportunity?

The three families (anyone else getting a mob vibe?) switched to a local Brethren church part way through Grade 4, and I was active in this church as well. There was no junior choir, but there were tween and youth groups held during the week where we did a lot of fun things like taking hikes on the Bruce Trail and holding awesome Halloween parties. None of my close friends attended the church except on the days when I'd coax them to attend this "kids crusade" event that was held at the church annually over five weekdays. There were songs and stories and challenges to memorize Bible verses that could earn you points. There were also points for bringing friends, and the more points your accrued, the bigger prize you could choose from the "treasure chest"—the biggest incentive to attend the crusade. I memorized some Bible verses, but I never won any of the big prizes mainly because, after the first visit, friends I invited knew I only wanted them there for the points, so they never returned.

The Brethren church was probably the best example of me wearing my "Christian hat" for an hour or so on Sundays and then changing into my "I'm-too-cool-for-Christianity hat" for the remaining 167 hours of the week. I believed in God, I prayed, I confessed my sins, and on the odd day I even "walked the talk." However, when my friends questioned me about "sensitive" issues like abortion, sex before marriage, and evolution, my responses were weak at best. I usually tried to change the subject, but I had one friend who wouldn't let me bow out that easily. She and her family members were science-minded atheists, and "For the Bible tells me so" didn't cut it.

Bad Temperance

For the first two years or so of high school, my friends and I did agree that underage drinking was wrong. Shawn was and remained a teetotaller throughout our teenage years (we lost touch in our mid-twenties when he moved to the States). I remember sitting with him on a bus during a school trip to visit the Royal Ontario Museum in Toronto. Two of my friends were sitting behind us and we overheard their conversation questioning why underage drinking and getting drunk was such a bad thing. Eventually, they decided they were going to give it a go at the next party. Shawn and I turned to each other with *There goes two more* looks on our faces.

But less than a year later, I joined the ranks. This is another thing Mom and Dad might be hearing for the first time, but I don't think they're going to gasp in disbelief. Nor will they fall off their chairs when they learn that I hosted several parties involving alcohol consumption from late in

Grade 11 through the beginning of Grade 13. Parents aren't as naïve as teenagers would like to believe.

The first time I gave into the drink was during a party at my house. Aside from Shawn, everyone was drinking to get drunk, and my drink of choice was rum and root beer (an appropriate name for it might be Barf on the Beach). I didn't puke, mainly because I was encouraged to drink a lot of water when I started to sober up, but I was the dancing queen, young and drunk, only seventeen.

I guess you could say I was a "happy drunk," whereas one of my friends was more of a "sad drunk." She would sit in a corner holding her knees to her chest. We played drinking games and there was a lot of loud talking and laughing. Just like everything was beautiful when Mr. Morphine visited, everything was funny when I was drunk. It was a good thing that we were living in rural Shelburne because if we had been at 2nd Avenue West, we would have definitely received complaints from the neighbours and maybe even a visit from the cops.

When I drank during a party at a friend's house, I either stayed overnight or until I felt sober enough to drive. I always made it home safely, and I was never stopped by the cops, but hindsight makes me wonder if I would have passed a breathalyzer test if I had been caught. What a different book I'd be writing if I had.

I can't honestly say that I didn't have fun during my drinking years. That's a double negative, so yes, I had a ton of fun. Parties weren't all drinking, however, as there were games and movies. Watching *Saturday Night Live* was the grand finale of most parties. It was a classic era for *SNL*, and I still remember many highlights.

Some of my friends had hot tubs and swimming pools, and we skated and snowmobiled in the winter. We were pretty good kids—no smoking, no drugs, no drunken fights, no major damage after a party. We did well in school and were active in many extracurriculars. Some of us paired up, broke up, paired up with someone else, but most of us were just friends with everyone.

And all the while, I was a Sunday Morning Christian, if that.

Dear Diary

Enter "the second time around." After writing the first part of this book, I recalled two journals that I kept from 1991 to 1993, after my BMT and during my struggles with Dr. P, HWMNBN and the Gang (in its acute days). I always kept the journals in boxes containing memorabilia, and I always came across them during apartment moves. The challenge was to find them and, as usual, they were in the last place I looked after practically tearing my apartment apart. No worries; it was worth the effort when I read some of the entries, the memories came flooding in.

I had copied several poems people sent or wrote me in the front and back covers of the journals, and while most of them were heartwarming and relevant to that time in my life, one stood out like a sore—no, mangled—thumb. This was a poem by L. E. Duncan called *I'm Not Alone* that I chose to be read during my baptism in the summer of 1987 when I was fifteen. I cringe because its theme is mostly opposite to the way I was living my life at the time (standing by your convictions despite being teased and labelled as odd). The poem isn't urging readers to ditch friends who don't share their faith, although it asks whether your friends were really your friends in the first place if they ditch you because of your faith.

Like I mentioned earlier, my high school friends and I were pretty good kids who supported, rather than judged, each other. However, I was ruled by my stupid pride, and I should have known that I didn't need to hide my faith. There's a big difference between judging someone's faith and questioning it, and while they sometimes challenged my beliefs, it didn't negatively affect our friendship. Part of this was likely because I didn't judge them for their views.

The journals had lists of several significant dates, like when I found out that I had relapsed, and I was able to clean up some details that I didn't have right in my first draft. But what caught my attention the most was how I was becoming less of a Sunday Morning Christian and more of a Walk the Talk Christian. Don't get me wrong, my walk the talks were still few and far between, but I was moving in a much better direction for my life despite frequently questioning God as to why I was "doomed to eternal ugliness" (the opening words of an entry on August 16, 1992) and living a life that was so vastly different from that of my friends and others around my age.

Sunny Days

The first entry in the first journal is on June 16, 1991 (I was nineteen), and it starts out with the words "What a special day!" I had a new Bible that offered a plan to not only read it in its entirety but in a way that I'd understand it and apply it to my life. In the next paragraph, I write about how I'd established June 6, 1991, as my "day of rebirth," when I'd sincerely begun to "take that step forward in my lagging walk with Jesus and never look back." The entry ends with me expressing my belief that I relapsed for a reason—so that I'd be "woken-up" and give my life to Jesus completely. Like all entries, I conclude with "Today's verses" and "Reading for today."

Entries over the next three and a half months are similar: Start with details of my day (I had an extremely active social life) and details of the body-related assaults from Dr. P and the Gang. I ask God to help me stop obsessing about my appearance and pray that His Will doesn't include things like the Gang becoming a chronic problem.

During the pre-HWMNBM days, my entries suggest I'm looking forward to attending university in the fall of 1991 ("I'm absolutely dying to go to university") and hoping that I'd find some Christian friends. I chastise myself for not acting like a Christian around my friends and write about how "some day my time will come and I'll meet that special guy." Verses I enter include those like Romans 8:28: "Even difficult experiences can be used in God's plan for good"; Joshua 1:5: "I will never leave you or forsake you"; Matthew 7:3: "Why do you look at the speck of sawdust in your brother's eye and pay no attention to the plank in your own eye." These are words I still regularly need to remind myself of.

Clouds Roll In

October 3 is the first entry that hints at HWMNBN's upcoming permanent residence in my body: "... it doesn't help much that I have a splitting headache today." Prior to HWMNBN, I rarely had headaches, and my "glass half empty" mind got me thinking that the headaches were a symptom of something much worse.

This time I was right.

The next entry isn't until December 2, and it opens with: "Remember that splitting headache I wrote about almost two months ago? Well, it was more—a lot more—and I still haven't recovered from it to this day." HWMNBN set a new, darker tone for several future entries. However, the final December 24 entry in the first journal ends on a positive and hopeful note: "I've been through a tough year, but God has gotten me through it and I pray that '92 is a year of healing and getting all of our lives back in swing again."

Entries in the second journal still end with relevant Bible verses and prayers for God's help in coping with the assault on my appearance and growing in my faith. However, fear and worries related to my health start to take up most of the space. While my social life remained relatively active, sometimes I got so worked up about my appearance that I made up excuses not to go out: "I've been getting myself down about my hair and my looks and my GvHD. I'm so afraid of facing my friends even though I know most of them won't care." Anything that I deemed out of the ordinary—a bruise, mouth sores not healing, stiff joints—became a sign that I was relapsing or I'd have to add more to the BABUDEEP chapter.

The tone of the second journal became especially dark when I entered university. It's interesting how my penmanship changes from neat to almost indecipherable on difficult days. The first entry, September 7, 1992, opens with, "Well, here I am at university. It's been a long time since I've been as terrified as I am now." The Bible verse for that day was, appropriately, "Be strong and courageous. Do not be terrified; do not be discouraged, for the Lord your God will be with you wherever you go." (Joshua 1:9)

When my mom and dad left after dropping me off at my student residence, I stayed in my room for the rest of the evening. I was worried about how I'd answer people if they asked me why I was in my room for so long but too afraid to go out and meet the other residents. I remember that day, but after reading some of what I wrote, I don't recall feeling quite so panicked: "I feel like a total freak and loser and

I just want to go home and hide ... I dread tomorrow and every day after that until at least Frosh Week is over." Golly gee willikers, sounds like I was about to run out the back door and hitch a ride home. The last words showed some semblance of positivity: "I really like my room, however, and I guess that's one good thing (the only one so far)." At least it showed that I chose not to hitch the ride.

Cloudy Morning, Sunny Afternoon

Things brightened up a little in the next two entries where I write about how I felt God guided me to InterVarsity Christian Fellowship and the Frosh Week activities they were offering where I met other Christians my age. However, this doesn't last, and soon I'm back to focusing on my insecurity, writing about how I skipped IVCF because I didn't feel comfortable, and how I "absolutely hate it here" and "don't know how I'm going to get through this year."

Enter my dad.

The September 11 entry rejoices over how I'm home for the weekend, but it also details a talk with my calm and rational dad, who is a master at shining a light on a difficult situation. He told me that I had to stop being so negative about myself and university. He said that this negativity would probably rub off on others and make them not want to be around me. He also encouraged me to focus on positive things in my situation.

My entry when I returned to university had a much brighter tone: "Well, I'm back again, but I'm feeling much better than I was feeling last Monday. I have the comfort of knowing that my brother and a good friend are here, and I've met two girls on my floor already who seem really nice."

My first two years of university were full of peaks and valleys—not making an effort to meet people; getting down on myself and feeling like I looked "half-decent"; worries about bumps and lumps and rejoicing over no more visits from Dr. P; high essay and low lab marks. However, my last three years took a turn for the better. By then, the Gang had waged war on my joints, muscles and tendons and I was back in student residence on a floor that had other occupants with varying disability types. I became close with two of the students, both with disabilities affecting their mobility, along with a few other able-bodied students. I was still insecure about my disability, but the discomfort mostly disappeared when I was around my new friends. I even started to hang out with people in my classes for the first time. By my final semester, I was rarely using the Student Access Van because I'd been working hard on regaining some mobility in my legs and was getting physiotherapy right on campus.

That Christian friend with a strong faith that I longed for remained elusive for almost fifteen years after I graduated university. I only had myself to blame because I didn't put much effort into finding her. My own faith wasn't strong enough to sense God's shoves in that direction. Well, that's not entirely true, it was more me closing myself off to His prompting. Pride and insecurity-related? You betcha! I decided that the friends I had were enough. As for fellowship with other Christians, I was close with my mom and dad, who were strong Christians, I attended a church group for post-secondary and graduate-aged peers, and some of the Christian friends Ted had were also my friends.

CHAPTER SIXTEEN:
THE TONIC OF SPECIAL FRIENDSHIPS

No Pain, No Gain

So how did that work out for you, you ask? My close non-Christian friends started drifting away, and before long, it was time for yearly Christmas cards. I made the search more difficult for myself when I didn't try hard enough to establish a strong bond with church group acquaintances before they started pairing up, marrying and having families. As a result, my family became my close Christian friends, but while I loved spending time with them, I knew that part of God's plan for our lives is to bless us with friendships outside of our families. I'm talking about friendships that God has a hand in, that were hand-picked and not developed due to random circumstances or coincidences.

    This is not to say that Christians should only have close friends who share their faith. I have a very close friend who is dear to me and we support each other and share personal things. She was the first person with whom I shared that I was writing this book, and she saw one of the earliest drafts. She doesn't share my strong faith, but we listen to what each other has to say about issues that can damage friendships when there's judgement and criticism involved. I've told her how I'd be the ultimate hypocrite to judge anyone, and she knows that one of my favourite Bible verses is the one about the speck in your eye and the plank in mine.

My efforts to find a close Christian friend grew stronger in my twenties, before I left my job as the programs director at a long-term care facility, although the growth was at a snail's pace. Our church had women's ministry groups open to anyone in the community, not just church attendees. Groups met once a week, and women could attend the day or early evening session (both if they were super keen). When my parents insisted that I at least try the evening group, I countered that I worked long hours and the last thing I wanted to do was go out again after I got home. The truth is that less than two hours a week was asking way too much of a lazybones like me.

I finally gave in, but not without a thick, heavy string attached. Among my mom's myriad responsibilities, she was helping out in the nursery while the ladies from the day group met. Even though I knew she had a lot on her plate, my "all about me" persona kicked into high gear and refused to go unless she went with me. The kind soul that she is, my mom relented and we began attending the early evening sessions.

The meetings were set up with around ten to twenty tables each seating six to eight women, including a leader. As a group, we sang a worship song, prayed and watched a video of the selected speaker on the big screen. Afterwards, table members would discuss the video and other topics, led by the table leader. There were three separate sessions per year with a break in the summer. For the first two years, you could call me "Violet," as I shrank away from others at the table and in the group as a whole. I demanded that we arrive just before the meeting started and leave immediately after—no socializing for me. I dreaded being asked by the table leader to read aloud or answer a question. Everyone seemed to know each other, and I made little to no effort to get to know anyone. This was just like Sunday mornings; I'd arrive at the church just before the service started (often five to ten minutes into the service) and leave right after. How could I possibly get to know anyone?

At the end of the evening, we'd have a quick look at the week's homework—mostly Bible verses and selected topics relevant to that week's talk, plus a lot of points to ponder related to our own lives. If you looked at my workbooks over the first two years, you'd see mostly blank pages. I wouldn't even take the ten to fifteen minutes every day to do the homework.

Sweet Friend of Mine

The third year was that glorious year when I met my first close Christian friend—hallelujah! My mom and I were placed at a table with three other women and a table leader with a strong southern accent that matched her equally strong personality. Sometimes you have an immediate connection with someone, no effort involved, and this was the case with Kathy. This meeting wasn't a coincidence, and I knew that while God was setting things in motion, I had to keep this friendship moving. God gave me another nudge when, at the end of the meeting, Kathy asked if I was available for lunch sometime in the coming days. Normally, I would have dipped into my ginormous bag of excuses, but I found myself excitedly agreeing and a date was set. Could it be that this was the first step in my metamorphosis from shrinking violet to social butterfly?

Lunch went great, and I found myself opening-up to Kathy about my long medical history. She opened-up about the peaks and valleys in her life as well, and we discovered that we shared a similar sarcastic sense of humour that has helped us get through difficult situations. She told me that she felt led by God to get to know me better and help me come out of my rock-hard, titanium-coated, quintuple-locked-and-chained shell. Most importantly, I now started not only looking forward to meetings, but I also did my homework. I began listening intently to the speakers and actively participating in the table talk. Seeing that my big baby persona was crumbling and I was entering into the big girl phase, my mom announced that she would no longer attend the evening sessions. Her plate was full and she needed to lighten the load.

My mom also became good friends with Kathy, no effort required between two social butterflies. In the summer of 2017, Kathy, my mom and I took a road trip to Lancaster, Pennsylvania, to do everything Amish. Lancaster's state-of-the-art Sight & Sound Theatre featured a two-thousand-seat auditorium and a massive three-hundred-foot panoramic stage that wrapped around the audience. The entertainment was designed to be universally appealing regardless of exposure to the Bible, and performances were based on Bible stories and always included live animals. *Jonah* (that whale-inhabiting dude again) was the performance we saw, and since I had phoned so far ahead to get tickets, I was given my choice of seats. I asked the person on the phone what she considered to be the best seats in the house, and her advice was right on the mark. When the virtual, life-sized whale made an appearance, I felt like I could reach out and touch it as it neared our section. It was my best theatre experience ever!

I think it was two years after we met that Kathy became one of the leaders of the women's evening ministry sessions, and she mentioned to her colleagues that I would also make a good leader. So there I was, the former indifferent, inactive introverted, now cordial, committed contributor helping to run the show. Kind of like a modern-day Jonah, except my decision *not* to run away from God's leading avoided the whale swallowing (not sure why I've had Jonah on the brain in this book, but his story is super cool, don'tcha think?).

Kathy and I were each other's closest Christian friends for more than a decade after. What a blessing it was to finally have a friend who shared my faith and agreed with me on everything pertaining to God and His Word, like all Christians do—said no one ever! Like everyone, we had differing views on many issues, and it was healthy to be challenged to look deeper into the topic. Maybe I'd change my mind. Maybe not. Maybe I'd find truth within both viewpoints. Anything that drove me to the Bible, had me praying for wisdom or asking questions of seasoned Christians was a good thing. If my research didn't change my mind, it didn't mean I hated the other person. Far from it. I respected her beliefs and hoped that she would mine as well.

Unfortunately, Kathy and her husband moved to Thunder Bay, which may as well be Mars it was so far away. The COVID-19 pandemic interrupted my plans to visit her, but emails, texts and phone calls worked OK. It was so comforting to know that she was just fingertips away!

CHAPTER SEVENTEEN:
FAITH, FRIENDSHIP AND GOD

That's What Friends Are For

Remember the Chronicles of Narnia series of seven books (*The Lion, the Witch and the Wardrobe* is probably the best known)? C. S. Lewis is the author of this series, and one particular quote from this book about friendship really stood out for me:

> ...Friendship is not a reward for our discriminating and good taste in finding one another out. It is the instrument by which God reveals to each of us the beauties of others.

Something else I've learned about friendship is how the care and compassion it involves, along with the comfort of knowing there's someone there for us, helps us to learn how we should treat others. In other words, we need to put the needs of others before our own needs. This is seeing others through God's eyes—how He cares for all of us equally and how we should treat others the way He treats us, even those we feel have done us wrong. This isn't easy, and I've always struggled with forgiveness, but I've learned that holding on to grudges and resentment does nothing but invite negativity.

My own insecurities started to encroach on my self-confidence around Grade 6. I matured a lot faster than the majority of my friends and peers, and the combination of puberty and my family's "bad skin genes" resulted in regular pizza deliveries to my face. On top of that, I had to get braces and my body was clearly entering the awkward stage. I probably would have been teased a lot more if I wasn't taller and stronger than most of my peers, including the boys.

"Tease me, and it's a knuckle sandwich for you!"

But seriously, the good friends God placed in my life kept me from being swallowed up by depression. For example, some fool once said that I should go buy some Preparation H.

"You idiot," one of my friends said, "You don't even know what Preparation H is for! Even my seven-year-old sister knows that!"

It was hilarious, but there always seemed to be something that I felt made me stand out in a negative way, which led to frequent rides on the "pity-party express." It was like a self-inflicted wound that I nurtured instead of trying to heal. At times, I would compare my life with the lives of family and friends that I viewed as superior to mine. Ted was (and sometimes still is) one of my regular targets. I saw his life as perfect: employed immediately after completing his post-secondary education; quickly moved up to supervisor and then upper management; happily married with four amazing kids; good health; loads of close Christian friends and others who look up to him. Unfortunately, we're no longer as close as we used to be, and I'm sure that, while I never voiced it when he was around, my resentment rubbed off on him. Who wants to be around that? I still take trips on the pity-party express, but Kathy and a few others God has placed in my life have greatly helped to shorten the rides.

The words and actions of these cherished friends when I start talking smack about myself show me how I need to keep seeing myself through God's eyes. My parents have been telling me this for decades, but sometimes it takes a non-family member—and in my case, people who haven't known me for my entire life—to get me to believe it. No one is totally honest with family or friends when they say something self-deprecating. I just counter with something like "Stop talking crazy, you're great at what you do and everyone thinks you're amazing, especially me." I'm not saying we should be brutally honest and agree with them: "Yeah, you're right, it must be hard to be such a failure," but I've learned that it's best not to use empty words.

Out of Focus

Joni Eareckson Tada's and Joyce Meyer's honest teachings have also helped to wire my brain to this truth. At the start of her conferences, Joyce has often said that if you came to be lifted up, you might want to exit immediately. Their audiences are not coddled and comforted by every message and teaching; instead they use "tough love." You may not like what they have to say, but you need to both hear and act on it if the situation is ever going to be resolved. We all need "rude awakenings" to get us back on the right track, but as the stubborn mule that I am, I need my weaknesses shouted out from the mountaintops to get me to listen. I have a tendency to balk at and become defensive in the face of criticism, warranted or not; however, I'm learning that knowing and accepting your weaknesses makes you stronger. Like it says in 2 Corinthians 12:9: "Therefore I will boast all the more gladly about my weaknesses, so that Christ's power may rest on me."

While I was editing the first draft of this book, I took a break and turned on an episode of Joyce's *Joy in Everyday Living* TV show. The topic was "If at First You Don't Succeed, You're Normal," and when I heard her say the words "Correction is not rejection, it's direction," I immediately grabbed my laptop, scrolled down to this section and added it.

She also talked about how most of us think that we're supposed to feel guilt. While she's not suggesting that it's OK to take our wrong actions lightly, she encourages us to replace guilt with acknowledging our mistakes, receiving God's grace, thanking Him that they were pointed out, and proactively learning from them. Otherwise, if you store up your guilt, you're more likely to keep repeating the same mistakes because simply acknowledging them isn't enough.

I wrote earlier about seeing ourselves through God's eyes, but I didn't explain what that meant. Four Bible translations use the words "handiwork" (NIV), "accomplishment" (CEB), "workmanship" (KJV), and "masterpiece" (NLT) in the first phrase of Ephesians 2:10 to describe what we are as God's creation. Whenever I get down on myself, it's so much easier to hold onto negative feelings like guilt and bitterness. In a May 17, 2021, website devotional, Joyce tells us that, "If we look at ourselves, at what we are in our own abilities, we cannot be anything except depressed and totally discouraged." A quote from Corrie ten Boom, the Christian woman I wrote about earlier who was sent to a concentration camp for hiding Jewish people, mirrors Joyce's words: "If you look at the world, you will be oppressed. If you look at yourself, you will be depressed. But if you look at Jesus, you will be at rest."

Turning my focus to Jesus has put me at rest throughout my journeys with The Big C. I vividly recall the peaceful feeling that enveloped me when I returned to my apartment after getting the confirmation of my stage 4 breast cancer diagnosis. I was sobbing and praying and questioning and emptying out all of my anger and disappointment to God. I've heard some people say they've heard God speak to them in difficult situations—not a, "Hey homey, chill out and listen while I lay out all the answers," kind of talk, rather a few quiet words of assurance and guidance. Although I didn't have this experience, I believe that God's non-verbal communication with me was just as miraculous. In the midst of my depression, He sent me a peace that assured me of His love.

Attitude is Latitude

Joni, the woman who broke her neck while diving, goes a step further in her September 13, 2021, podcast entitled "Enduring with a Grateful Spirit." She speaks of how it takes faith to face a trial, but it takes endurance to keep embracing that trial. Romans 15:5 speaks of how God gives endurance and encouragement; however, this is an offer, not a freebie. Our response in times of suffering— begrudging or heartfelt and hopeful—determines whether or not we receive this offer. Joyce states in her September 25, 2021, online devotional that, "When you decide to act in favour of God's ways, He also joins forces with you."

This may sound easy, but it's not. As you may surmise, I lean towards a "glass half empty" mentality and tend to think the worst even at a relatively minor occurrence. But I find myself pitching my tent on the sunny side of the street more often when I choose God's help in enduring hard times with a hopeful spirit. And like Joni writes in her previously mentioned podcast, "It changes your life, it changes your outlook, and best of all, it changes your heart."

One of my mom's close friends, a strong Christian woman who also struggled with The Big C and passed away from it in her early sixties, visited me one day not long after I was sprung from the joint the first time around. I was lounging on a lawn chair outside and don't recall everything she said, but she was comforting, and I really appreciated her praying with me. One thing she said has stayed with me to this day. She said that God told her He had something special planned for my life. I waited for something spectacular and out of the ordinary to happen for about a decade, but nothing seemingly did. Over the following decades I've thought about her words every now and then and usually made light of them.

"Yay, I'm now a 'person with a disability.' Woo-hoo, a new Big C diagnosis—my special blessing has finally arrived!"

I'm ashamed of this flippant thinking, as I wasn't considering that God allows (not causes) difficult things in our life to redirect our thoughts, words and actions towards Him. Joyce writes in her October 4, 2021, online devotional: "Your attitude is your thought life turned inside out." It's far too easy for me to cloak my disappointment in sarcasm and cynicism, forgetting how God can take the hurts and wounds I endure and use them for good in both my life and the lives of others. Perhaps God's special blessing for my life is writing this book, getting it published and distributed, and touching readers in some positive way. Maybe I'm going to get miraculously healed or live much longer than expected. Or perchance, my faith will continue to grow consistently instead of in peaks and valleys, and when I face God at the pearly gates, He'll say, "Well done, my precious daughter and servant." I'll take curtain #3, God, but if you happen to give me curtain #1 and/or #2 as well, I won't complain.

It's easier for me to write this knowing that I currently have no pain or serious side effects from my Big C-killing meds. My mantra used to deflect pity is still relevant: "I can live independently, drive and work full-time." And, "incurable" diagnosis or not, every moment we have is a gift from God. However, I'm well aware that believing in something and acting on it are not symbiotic—certainly not for a lazybones like me.

I know what I'm facing, and I have met and read about people whose treatments are no longer working. Their downhill battle that they eventually lose scares me, especially when it happens at a young age. Pondering rather than obsessing on this reality helps me to make a conscious effort to make my days productive and meaningful. So, will I still choose curtain #3 or make light of my current diagnosis as I've often done in this book if or when The Big C takes over? I know in my heart that curtain #3 can stand on its own. However, the heart and the mind don't always agree.

Crashing the Pity Parties

Sure, there are more times than I'd like to admit when I worry about my diagnosis shortening my life by a few decades. Waiting for what seems like an eternity to get test results can turn my thoughts to the cancer spreading around my body. However, it's only the times when I stop or put off praying and reading God's Word that the calm and contentment wanes. I can crash the pathetic petty pity parties when I switch my focus to the multitude of blessings God has given and continues to give me. It also helps when I turn my thoughts to those who suffer so much more and have so much less than I do, including people who would be thankful just to have a roof over their heads, one decent meal each day and access to even the most basic health care.

Another way to turn my back when my "all about me" facade rears its ugly mug is to think about Joni. Now in her early seventies, her quadriplegia has caused increasing and often debilitating chronic pain on top of a stage 3 breast cancer diagnosis and the extra pain treatment adds. I've read and heard her speak many times over the years of how she thanks God for her accident, saying, "I'd rather be in this wheelchair knowing Him than on my feet without Him." After the accident, Joni sank into a deep depression and even lost the will to live. But it was when she chose to change her attitude from begrudging to heartfelt and hopeful, accepting and leaning on God's courage and strength, that she could truthfully speak these words.

Thinking about how Joni still hosts her own pity parties and that she crashes them by turning her thoughts away from herself encourages me to do the same. I can't even fathom what it would be like to live with intense pain 24/7, and it's when I'm on my figurative knees, humbled to the core, that I recall how God never promised that those who accept Him into their hearts are in for an easy life that is free from pain and suffering. But He did promise that He will never give us more than we can bear and that He will guide us through the darkness into the light. A comforting phrase my mom often used during the particularly difficult times I faced throughout my first two journeys with The Big C was, "This too shall pass." And it always did.

Joyce used this phrase in her online devotional, where she refers to 1 Corinthians 4:17-18:

> "Seasons of difficulty always pass. They do not last forever.
>
> Going though trials is tough, but God is always with us, helping us, encouraging us, and fighting our battles for us. He never wants us to stay in pain. He always wants to heal us.

This is spiritual healing, the kind I'm experiencing as I write these words. However, I'm also thinking about how often I still give in to worldly temptations and search for contentment in material things. It's kind of like the way I waited so long to do something about the lump I found in my right breast that turned out to be stage four breast cancer; the time to be proactive about my lagging faith is now, especially when I know that waiting will only make finding peace in difficult times and joy in everyday living less attainable.

EPILOGUE

Tying Up Loose Ends

Well, my story ends here. Thanks for sticking it out with me through my journeys with the 2nd Avenue Gang, the first and second times around, the Zonk, Dr. P, HWMNBN and the Gang from the BABUDEEP, the caregiver shout-outs, the GOATs (Greatest of All Time) and WOATS (Worst of All Time).

OK, so what about how I used the tapestry metaphor a few chapters back? As I understood it, a tapestry is a piece of thick fabric with pictures or designs that are formed by weaving coloured weft threads or by embroidering on canvas. They are often used as a wall hanging or a furniture covering.

And that's the image most people have.

But digging a little deeper, I found an additional meaning that provides a good representation for the foundation of this book. Tapestry can also mean an intricate or complex combination of things or sequence of events. It's not just a wall hanging! I see God as the thread that has woven love, grace and mercy into every sequence of events within my journey with The Big C. I envision myself as the artist who needs to have patience with the thread and faith that, while my tapestry may look like a hot mess right now, it will emerge as a thing of beauty in the end. How's that for an explanation? You know the answer: Not so bad if I do say so myself!

AFTERWORD

I'm not sure who's gonna read this. If I'm the only one, it'll be worth it because jumping on the time machine of my life has been cathartic. As I wrote, humorous details kept popping into my head that I used to lighten up my story. Including the difficult memories was important as it became clearer than ever how going through turbulent times makes me a better person.

I decided to start writing about my life because it has been a roller coaster. Maybe it is more like the ones in kiddieland compared to what my mentors Joni and Joyce have gone through, but there have still been a number of twists and turns that made for an interesting story. If I'm gonna use clichés, I might as well add that if my story ends up reaching beyond those who know me best, I hope that you enjoyed the ride. Even if your feelings were more along the lines of *meh*, I thank you for sticking it out to the end.

Most importantly, I pray that God has spoken to you through my story and ignited a spark—or at least some questions. Joyce has mentioned in her teachings and devotionals how she's looking forward to going to heaven, but what a greater joy it is knowing she's had a part in others joining her.

What a blessing!

The End.

ACKNOWLEDGEMENTS

Armed with God's tools of love and wisdom, my parents built a strong foundation for my life. More times than I'd like to admit, my decisions and actions took a jackhammer to this foundation, but I am thankful I was never able to completely destroy it. Parents find joy in watching their children grow and succeed in life. For a Christian parent, the greatest joy is watching their children grow in the Lord. In their later years, my parents continue to face serious health-related challenges, but they're always put on the back-burner when similar challenges surface in the life of their almost fifty-year-old daughter.

Mom and Dad, my life has been filled with your gifts. In return, I want to give you the gift of knowing that I'm growing stronger in the Lord every day and you've played an integral role in keeping me from slipping backwards. I love you!

Addendum

Although moved to tears, I would be remiss not to mention the many others who have contributed to the publication of this book.

First and foremost are the members of Sarah's family. Her mom provided ongoing support, her niece contributed some creative elements the book needed, and I who determined that this book would be published and worked with professionals from Tellwell Publishing to make this happen.

I would especially like to mention Sarah's niece Breanne, who designed the cover of the book, wrote the medical disclaimer and provided ongoing support and encouragement.

Without the supportive Tellwell staff, this book would have never gone beyond a dream. Special thanks go to Darin, who guided me through the editing process that resulted in a slimmer yet more impactful volume; to Colleen, who guided me through the intricacies of marketing; to Shaira, who coordinated the process, prevented me from becoming overwhelmed and kept me on track. I have learned so much!

Finally, I thank God for giving us almost fifty-two years with Sarah. He used her life to show us what real persistence and hope look like. And He enabled this book—as Sarah wrote it and as the publishing process has given it shape.

ABOUT THE AUTHOR

Sarah Murray seemed to have an idyllic childhood. Then, at age 14, it all came tumbling down. For the next 37 years she dealt with the impacts of cancer. And she did so in a way that encompassed what it means to be a "hero".

Made in the USA
Middletown, DE
05 July 2024